P9-CMK-302

ICE HOCKEY MADE SIMPLE: A SPECTATOR'S GUIDE

THIRD EDITION

by P.J. Harari and Dave Ominsky

Illustrated by Anna Mendoza and Stephen J. Lattimer

Cover design by Eugene Cheltenham

Photographs © by Bruce Bennett Studios

© 1998, 1996, 1993 First Base Sports, Inc.,
Los Angeles, California
http://www.firstbasesports.com

JUN 3 0 1999

Look for these other Spectator Guides:
- Basketball Made Simple
- Football Made Simple
- Soccer Made Simple

Also published by First Base Sports:
- How To Win a Sports Scholarship

© 1998, 1996, 1993 First Base Sports, Inc.,
Los Angeles, California

ISBN 1-884309-09-7
Library of Congress Catalog Card Number: 98-71526

We welcome your comments and questions:
FIRST BASE SPORTS, INC.
P.O. BOX 1731
MANHATTAN BEACH, CALIFORNIA 90267-1731
(310) 318-3006

Typesetting by Jelico Graphics

Photographs provided in this publication are for editorial illustration only and do not indicate any affiliation between the publishers of this book and the National Hockey League, its teams, or its players or Players' Association.

HOW TO USE THIS BOOK

The sport of hockey is booming in popularity as it develops a more diverse audience which includes more families than ever -- both in the U.S. and Canada. The growing fascination with hockey is reflected in merchandise sales -- one of the top logos in <u>all</u> sports today belongs to the Anaheim Mighty Ducks! There is even the spin-off sport of roller hockey which is the hottest new game in the nation. So many new fans, yet few of them are able to fully understand the exciting sport of hockey.

This book aims to educate anyone who wants to know more about this exciting game. It is written for use by a variety of audiences — adults who want to become fans, children who want to learn the basics of the sport they are playing and even existing fans who want a quick reference guide to their favorite sport.

Each chapter has been written to stand alone, so you do not have to sit and read the book from cover to cover. However, the chapters do build on each other, so if you start at page 1 and read through to the end, the chapters flow logically and become more detailed as you progress.

This book will mainly discuss the rules of ice hockey as played at the professional level in the United States. Rules, as well as any word or phrase printed in *italics*, can be referenced quickly and easily using the book's glossary or index. So get ready to learn about ice hockey, America's most exciting sport.

HOCKEY ORGANIZATIONS

PROFESSIONAL MAJOR LEAGUE
National Hockey League (NHL): Organized in 1917, the NHL has grown to 27 teams divided into 2 *conferences* (with 3 *divisions* each). Currently, 6 of its teams are in Canada and the rest are in the United States as the league continues to expand into non-traditional hockey markets such as the Southeastern U.S. The league expects to add another 3 *expansion teams* by the year 2000. Its teams play an 82-game *regular season* from October to April, then *playoffs* to compete for the *Stanley Cup*.

PROFESSIONAL MINOR LEAGUES
Ten professional *minor leagues* (with a total of over 150 teams) each develop talent for the NHL or higher-level minor leagues. Three of these leagues have clubs directly *affiliated* with an NHL team. Players on an affiliated club *roster* can be called up to the NHL at any time during the season. Of the leagues discussed below, the IHL and AHL feed players directly to the NHL, while the ECHL, CHL, UHL and WCHL are a step lower, providing players to the IHL and AHL.

Each of these minor leagues follows its own set of rules, although most rules are similar to those followed by the NHL. One exception is the use of a *shootout* instead of *overtime* to resolve *ties* by almost all the minor leagues. Some leagues use a combination of overtime *period*(s) followed by a shootout. A shootout is when teams alternate turns taking *penalty shots* at one *goal* defended by the opposing *goalie*. A different player must take each shot until a team runs out of players. The winner is the team that has the most goals after 5 shots are taken by each team. If the game is still tied (each team has scored on an equal number of shots), the shootout continues with alternating penalty shots until one team scores and the other team does not (sudden-death).

International Hockey League (*IHL*): Founded in 1945 and headquartered in Detroit (formerly in Indianapolis), this league is the highest level below the NHL, has the advantage of being in the biggest markets of any minor league (e.g., Chicago, Detroit, Houston, Los Angeles) and was the first to break the 3 million attendance mark in a single season. In the 3 seasons from 1995-1998, over 17 million spectators attended IHL games! The IHL has 17 teams in 2 conferences (with 2 divisions each). While most IHL teams operate as independent clubs, others have varying contractual agreements with the NHL to provide players.

The teams play an 82-game season followed by a 4-round *playoff* format where teams compete for the Turner Cup. Instead of *overtime*, the IHL was the first league to use a *shootout system* to resolve *ties* — teams receive 2 *points* for a win, 0 for a loss, and 1 for a loss after a shootout. The IHL plays more veterans than the other minor leagues with an average age of 26. Of all players, 70% are Canadian, 20% are American and 10% are European. The first woman to play in a professional hockey game, Marion Rhume, did so in a 1992 IHL game.

American Hockey League (*AHL*): This league has 19 teams (4 Canadian and 15 in the United States) which play an 80-game regular season, and one more U.S. team is being added for 1999-00. Its *playoffs* lead to the Calder Cup. The AHL does not use a shootout system to resolve *ties*, instead using the same rules as the NHL. After a 5-minute sudden-death *overtime period*, a game is declared a tie during the *regular season*. During the playoffs, the teams play continuous sudden-death overtime periods until a winner is determined. This league is more developmental than the IHL; of its 22-player roster a team must dress 10 players with less than 260 NHL, AHL or IHL games of experience. Founded in 1936, it is headquartered in West Springfield, Massachusetts.

East Coast Hockey League (*ECHL*): The second-largest hockey circuit after the NHL is also the largest developmental hockey league in North America for players, coaches, officials and front-office talent. The ECHL has 27 teams in 1998-99 (with 2 more slated to join in 1999-00) stretching from New Orleans to Miami to Trenton, NJ to Peoria, IL. Beginning in 1997-98, the ECHL split into 2 *conferences* (Northern and Southern) and 4 *divisions* (Northwest, Northeast, Southwest and Southeast). After a 70-game season that begins in mid-October, *playoffs* begin in early April. The playoff format is the same as the NHL's, with the top 8 teams in each conference qualifying for the playoffs. These teams compete for the Kelly Cup (named in 1996-97 after the league's only commissioner, Pat Kelly; formerly called the Jack Riley Cup). The ECHL uses a shootout system to resolve ties only during the regular season. During the playoffs 20-minute sudden-death *overtime* periods are played until a goal is scored.

Each team has a maximum of 18 players and a *salary cap* of $8,000 per week ($450 per player average). Each team can have a maximum of 4 players that have played 200 professional games, called veterans. Founded in 1988, it is headquartered in Princeton, New Jersey.

Central Hockey League (*CHL*): The original CHL, started in 1963, became defunct in 1984. Re-formed in 1992, this 10-team league is now headquartered in Indianapolis, Indiana. For its first 4 seasons the new league owned all its teams, but there are currently 5 independent franchises in the CHL's two divisions. Once centered in Texas, Oklahoma, Kansas and Tennessee, the CHL expanded east into Alabama, North Carolina and Georgia. After a 70-game regular season that opens in late-October, 8 teams go to the playoffs in late-March. The league uses a shootout system during the regular season, switching to continuous sudden-death overtime periods to resolve ties during the playoffs. Team rosters are limited to 18 players (17 dress for a game) whose salaries average $500 per week.

United Hockey League (UHL): Formerly the *Colonial Hockey League* until 1997, the UHL plays a 74-game season that lasts from October to March. The league consists of 11 teams in Michigan, New York, Illinois, Wisconsin, North Carolina and Ontario, Canada, and plans to add two more teams for the 1999-00 season. To maintain balance among teams, league rules require each team to have at least 3 *rookies* but no more than 8 veterans on its roster. The UHL is headquartered in Saint Louis, Missouri.

West Coast Hockey League (WCHL): Established in 1995 and based in Boise, Idaho, the WCHL has 10 teams that compete across 7 states and 3 time zones. Its 64-game season starts in October and culminates in the Taylor Cup Championship playoffs in April. Although league rules limit each team's salary total to just $10,000 per week, players are often "called up" to play in the more prestigious IHL during the season. WCHL attendance exceeded 1 million fans in a season for the 1st time in 1998.

Western Professional Hockey League (WPHL): This rapidly growing league started in 1996 and has established teams in the "non-traditional" hockey markets of the Southwest, Texas and the Deep South. The addition of 5 expansion teams in 1998 gives the WPHL a total of 17. Teams play from October to March followed by playoffs, with the champion taking home the President's Cup.

Canadian Hockey League: This organization actually consists of 3 minor leagues in Canada and the Northwest United States – the Western Hockey League (18 teams in Western Canada and the Northwest U.S.), the Ontario Hockey League (18 teams in Ontario), and the Quebec Major Junior Hockey League (15 teams in Quebec). These leagues provide much of the talent chosen in the annual NHL entry *draft*.

ROLLER HOCKEY LEAGUES

Many IHL and AHL hockey players also play roller hockey in the off-season to sharpen their skills. This newer sport is played by players wearing rollerblades on a "Sport Court", a plastic surface with no blue lines that allows the fire-red puck they use to move even faster than on ice. The speed of the puck combined with teams of only 5 players to a side creates a higher-scoring game. Each game is divided into four 12-minute quarters.

Major League Roller Hockey (MLRH): Headquartered in Florence, South Carolina, the MLRH started in 1997 with 8 teams and expanded to a total of 20 by 1998. Fourteen teams are in the North American Conference and play in the U.S., while the other 6 teams play in the United Kingdom's World Conference. The season lasts from June to August followed by a World Championship Series held at the Arrowhead Pond in Anaheim, California. To promote hometown heroes, the league requires that each team of 20 players (14 active) must include 4 players that live within 100 miles of its home arena.

Roller Hockey International (RHI): This first-ever professional roller hockey league founded in 1993 took its 6th season off in 1998 to reorganize its financial structure. RHI expects to resume its 10-week summer season in 1999 with 10 to 12 teams and to grow steadily by 2 teams each year thereafter. A unique compensation structure closely ties player salaries to team performance during the regular season and playoffs. The RHI is headquartered in Denver, Colorado.

TABLE OF CONTENTS

The Origins of Hockey 1
The Object of Ice Hockey 2
The Hockey Rink 3
Uniforms & Equipment 8
How The Game Is Played 13
    Length of the Game... 13
    Trying to Score Goals 14
    Defense 16
    Starting Play: Face-offs 18
    Stopping Play 19
The Team & Player Positions 21
Team & Individual Scoring 28
The Officials 30
Penalties 33
Things To Look For During Play / Strategy 46
NHL Teams, Divisions and Conferences 53
NHL Season, Playoffs and The Stanley Cup 56
Individual Statistics 63
Deciphering Hockey Statistics In The Newspaper 65
NHL Individual Records 68
The NHL Draft 74
NHL All-Star Game & Teams 76
The Hockey Hall Of Fame 78
NHL Hockey Trophies 79
Hockey Personalities: Past And Present 84
Glossary 106
Index 119
Officials' Hand Signals.. 123

THE ORIGINS OF HOCKEY

No one is quite sure where hockey began. Several countries claim they invented the sport—the Irish game of hurley bears a close resemblance, while the French claim the name is derived from the French word *hoquet* (shepherd's crook). A similar game, hockie, was played in Galway as far back as 1527.

North American ice hockey most likely originated in Canada, where, it is rumored, soldiers began to informally pass a ball around on the ice. In 1879, W.F. Robertson and R.F. Smith, two students at Montreal's McGill University, tried to adapt field hockey to ice and devised the first official rules and regulations. Not surprisingly, the first team to play by these prearranged rules was the McGill University Club during the 1880-81 season.

The Amateur Hockey Association of Canada was formed around 1889, and by the turn of the century there were many teams in assorted leagues. The National Hockey Association was formed in 1910; it was the forerunner of the *National Hockey League* (NHL) which was formed in 1917.

The game was first played with a wooden disk, which was later replaced with a more durable rubber lacrosse ball. This worked well outdoors, but in indoor games the bouncing ball broke windows. Today's flat *puck* was born when a frustrated *rink* owner, trying to prevent further damage, took a knife and sliced off the top and bottom of the ball. Many such equipment changes and rule changes have characterized the evolution of hockey since the NHL began.

THE OBJECT OF ICE HOCKEY

The simplest explanation of ice hockey is to say it is a fast-paced game played on a frozen ice surface by two teams of 6 players each. These players wear *skates* and carry a wooden *stick* that curves at the bottom. They use the sticks to push the playing piece, called a *puck*, across the ice and into a *net* to score *points*, which are called *goals*. The object of the game is for each team to try to score more goals than its opponent.

The principle guiding the rules of hockey is that of continuous action. Only the *officials* can stop the game and then only under certain circumstances. If a player has personal difficulties, such as a minor injury, wanting or needing a rest, having his shorts fall off while on the ice, or even breaking his stick, he must deal with these problems while the game continues.

Keeping this simple summary of the game in mind, you can now review each of the sections describing the rules, strategies and player positions to get a more complete view of ice hockey. Most of the rules are quite logical, stemming from a desire to *keep the game moving* while trying to *protect players* from serious injury. If you remember these two overall concerns in hockey, you will have little trouble understanding the rules of the game.

Ice hockey is an exciting game, and once you learn its relatively simple rules, you will be well on your way to enjoying this spectacular sport.

THE HOCKEY RINK

Ice hockey is played on an indoor ice surface called a *rink*, located inside an arena. (See **Figure 1**) Each professional team has its own arena located in its home city, and while there are some differences between the arenas (such as the seating capacity), the similarities are vast.

The rink size is 200 feet long and 85 feet wide with rounded corners. Only a handful of current *NHL* arenas have rinks that vary in size from these dimensions. Wooden or fiberglass walls surround the rink to protect the fans and prevent the *puck* (and the players) from accidentally leaving the area. These walls, called *boards*, are approximately 3 ½ feet high; they are more specifically called *sideboards* along the length of the rink and *endboards* behind the *goals*. Today, rinks also have shatterproof glass that rises above the boards to provide even greater protection from flying pucks.

Lines are drawn on the ice and another layer of ice is frozen over them. These lines are continued and drawn up along the boards as well. The diagram on the next page might help you to picture these better.

- *Blue lines* divide the ice into three equal sections; these are called the *defending zone,* the *attacking zone* and the *neutral zone* in between them.

- A red *center line* divides the ice surface in half; it is located in the neutral zone, between the two blue lines.

- Two red *goal lines* are located 13 feet in from the endboards, one at each end of the rink. This distance was increased from 11 feet in 1998 to increase scoring opportunities by giving *passers* more room to maneuver behind the *net*.

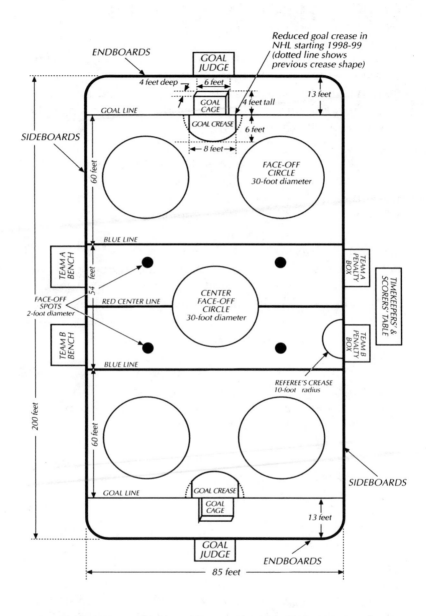

Figure 1: A hockey rink.

Centered on each red goal line is a *goal cage*. (See **Figure 2**) The goal cage consists of a tubular frame, two *goalposts* joined at the top by a metal *cross bar*, 4 feet high and 6 feet wide. It is through this opening that the puck must pass to score a goal. When a goal is scored, a red light located behind the goal is turned on to show that a team has made a point. A net, made of white nylon cord, is draped over and attached to the frame to reduce the chance of the puck coming out or passing through without being detected as a goal; it extends back about 4 feet. This entire area is often referred to as the goal or the *net*.

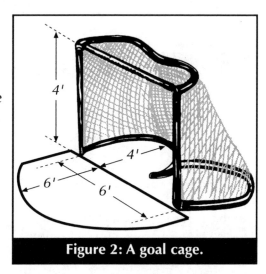

Figure 2: A goal cage.

Drawn on the ice in front of the goal is the *goal crease*, a semi-circular area with a 6 foot radius. An attacking player may only enter this area when the puck is in the crease but no goal can legally be scored while he remains there. The size of the NHL's crease was reduced near the corners of the goal starting with the 1998-99 season to lower the number of goals disallowed because of crease infractions. One player from each team stands in the goal crease in front of each goal to protect it; he is called the *goalie*. Any player can skate in the area behind each net because it is part of the rink.

The neutral zone is neutral for both teams, but the attacking and defending zones are different for each team. Each team defends its own goal. The team's goalie, therefore, stays near its goal and tries to prevent the puck

5

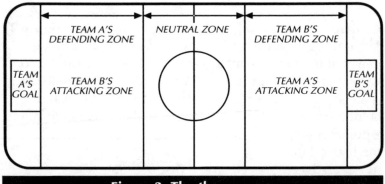

Figure 3: The three zones.

from being placed there by the other team. The goalie and goal are both in the team's defending zone, which is the attacking zone for the other team. **An easy way to remember it is to think: Team A is trying to stop, or** *defend*, **the** *attack* **of Team B. Therefore, we are in Team A's** *defending* **zone and Team B's** *attacking* **zone.** At the opposite end of the ice is Team B's goal and Team B's defending zone which is also Team A's attacking zone. Here, Team B tries to stop, or defend, the attack of Team A. As you can see, one team's defending zone is always the other team's attacking zone. (See **Figure 3**)

There are also several circles and other lines drawn on the ice. The circles are used by the *referee* or *linesman* to put the puck back into play and start the action again whenever it has stopped, through a procedure called a *face-off* which is discussed in the chapter on **HOW THE GAME IS PLAYED.** Altogether, there are 9 circles and 3 semi-circular areas drawn on the ice:

- The large blue circle in the middle of the rink is called the *center face-off circle.*

- There are four red *face-off spots* in the neutral zone.

- Two more red *face-off circles* are located at each end of the rink near the goal lines.

- Two semi-circular areas, one in front of each goal, are called the goal creases and denote the playing areas of each goalie, into which no attacking player without the puck may enter.

- A semi-circular area with a 10-foot radius in front of the *timekeepers' table* is the *referee's crease*, an area into which no player may enter or follow the referee.

On one side of the rink, behind the sideboards, there are two team *benches*, one for each of the teams. Although only 6 players are on the ice at one time, there are usually 20 players on a team.

The others sit on the bench until it is time for them to substitute for players on the ice. Since they need to skate onto the ice quickly to substitute, these benches are located just off the ice behind the sideboards. The coaches, managers and team trainers also sit on this bench throughout the game. The *timekeepers* and *official scorer* sit at a special table located on the same side as, and in between, the two *penalty boxes*.

There are also penalty benches located in two penalty boxes where players are sent to sit for a specified period of time after they have broken a rule (committed a *penalty*). A player will sit in the penalty box until his penalty time is up (expires), and then he will rejoin his team. The penalty box is also located behind the sideboards, but across the ice from the team benches.

Now let us see what **UNIFORMS & EQUIPMENT** players use.

UNIFORMS & EQUIPMENT

Professional hockey players wear special uniforms and ice skates with boots. Each player carries a stick to move the puck. (See **Figure 4**) Goalies use different equipment from the rest of the players.

STICKS

Hockey players use L-shaped wooden, aluminum, graphite or fiberglass *sticks* which are viewed as two connected parts: the handle, or shaft, curves around into the bottom part called the blade. The area where the shaft and blade meet is called the heel. Sticks can be a maximum of 63 inches long measured from the heel to the end of the shaft. The blade must not exceed 12 ½ inches in length and must be between 2 and 3 inches in height; it must have beveled edges. The blade can have a very slight curve (limited to ½ inch) or can be angled to the left or the right. Most hockey players go through several sticks a season and have sticks that suit their particular style of playing. Adhesive tape may be wrapped around the stick at any place for the purpose of reinforcement or to improve the handling of the stick; use of tape will also vary with individual players.

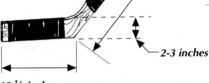

STICK

63 inches max.

1 inch **PUCK**

3 inches

2-3 inches

12 ½ inches max.

Figure 4: Stick and puck.

Goalies carry slightly different sticks than the other players: the shaft must have a knob of adhesive tape at least $^1/_2$ an inch thick at the top and the blade measures 15 $^1/_2$ by 3 $^1/_2$ inches. Unlike a player who can skate to his bench to replace a broken stick, the goalie must wait for a teammate to bring him a new stick from the bench or else he incurs a *penalty*.

PUCK
Hockey is played with a vulcanized hard rubber disk called a *puck*, 1 inch thick and 3 inches in diameter, weighing 6 ounces. To reduce the bounce of the rubber and to increase their speed to over 100 miles per hour, pucks are frozen before each game and changed throughout the game.

SKATES AND BOOTS
Each player wears special ice hockey skates with very sharp steel blades that are *rockered*, or curved up at the front and back. (See **Figure 5**) Rockered blades make it easier for players to start and turn quickly. Blades are sharpened for each game. For protection,

Figure 5: Skates and boots.

boots are strong, heavily padded shoes; the padding extends up around the ankle. The boots of goalies and *defensemen* are stronger than those of the *forwards*. It is not unusual for a professional player to wear out or break several pairs of skates each season.

NON-GOALIE EQUIPMENT & UNIFORMS
Defensemen and forwards wear the same basic protective padded clothing and uniform. (See **Figure 6**) They start with special perspiration absorbing underwear, and a garter belt attached to long woolen, footless stockings which cover hard plastic padded shin guards. Under a

9

loose-fitting team jersey and knee-length nylon shorts held up by suspenders, they wear a long sweater, shoulder pads with rib protection attached, elbow pads, and a supporter especially designed for the rough action of hockey. Their shorts act as a girdle and have built-in pads to protect their hips, thighs and the area near their kidneys. Defensemen may add ankle guards to prevent bruising or breakage. All the players wear padded gauntlet *gloves* with big cuffs to protect the arm up to the elbow. These gloves cannot have holes in them that would allow fingers to protrude and be used to hold onto or grab an opponent's uniform.

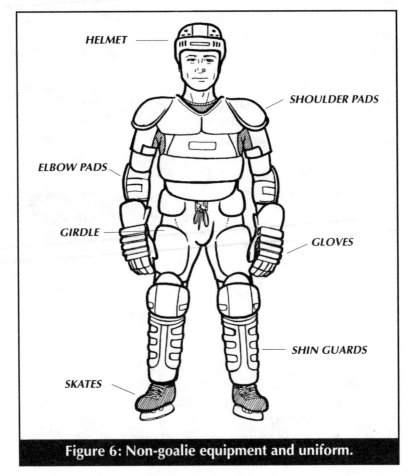

Figure 6: Non-goalie equipment and uniform.

The team jersey is generally white for home games and dark for games played *on the road*. This makes it easier to distinguish teams. On the front of the jersey is the team emblem and on the back is the player's name and number. When a player is the team *captain*, a three-inch C is on the front; a three-inch A denotes the alternate captain(s).

GOALIE UNIFORMS
Goalies start with the same basic uniform as their teammates, but they wear additional protective clothing weighing up to 40 pounds more. Instead of shin guards they wear large pads, 3-4 inches thick, around each leg from the ankle to the thighs, and they also wear pads on their shoulders, arms and chest. The padding in their pants is also thicker than that of their teammates. A goalie uses two different kinds of gloves, one for each hand. The glove for the hand that holds his stick is made of padded leather and has a large rectangular pad attached to the front of it; it is called the *waffle pad*. It is used to knock the puck away when it is shot at his goal. On the other hand he wears a catching glove, with which he can scoop up the puck and hold it or drop it away from the goal. Even goalies' skates are different; they are heavier than those of their teammates and there is almost no open space between the skate blade and the bottom of the skate to prevent the puck from accidentally passing through the skate and into the goal. Finally the goalie wears a hard helmet as well as a mask that covers his face.

HEAD GEAR
Players were not always required to wear a *helmet*. Today, helmets are mandatory equipment for all NHL players, although as recently as 1997, certain veteran players who had never played with one were exempted from the rule. The helmet is a light weight, plastic-padded head protector with ventilation holes and slots so that the player's head does not get too warm. The goalie wears a hard helmet as well as a mask that covers his face.

ZAMBONI

The machine used to clean the ice and smooth it out is called a *Zamboni,* named after its inventor, Frank Zamboni. It will make an appearance before the start of every *period,* taking about 10 minutes to clean the ice. Since the 1994-95 season, the NHL requires that 2 Zamboni machines be used to clean the surface.

EQUIPMENT VIOLATIONS

Whenever a team believes a player on the other team is playing with equipment that is not regulation dimensions (for example a blade with too much curvature), a formal complaint can be made to the referee by the captain or alternate captain. The *referee* will take the suspicious equipment to the *timekeeper,* who will make the necessary measurement and report it to the *penalty timekeeper* who records it. If the complaint is justified, the player committing the infraction is assessed a *minor penalty* and fined. If it is not, the team that requested the measurement is penalized. A goalie may not wear extra equipment, and players are not permitted to wear anything the officials consider dangerous to himself or to other players. No non-goalie player is allowed to wear a mask (unless he has a broken facial bone).

Now let us see **HOW THE GAME IS PLAYED**.

HOW THE GAME IS PLAYED

Five of the 6 players on each team skate around the ice trying to put the playing piece, called a *puck*, into the *net* to score *points*, called *goals*. The team that has the most goals at the end of the game is the winner.

LENGTH OF THE GAME

In the *NHL*, each game has three 20-minute *periods*. A large clock counts down the minutes and seconds of playing time and shows the players and fans how much time is left in each period. The clock is stopped when the playing stops, and started up again when the playing resumes. In between each period there is a 15-minute *intermission*. So each professional hockey game has 3 periods of play and 2 intermissions, lasting a minimum of 90 minutes. This is called a *regulation* game. However, a game always takes much longer than 90 minutes to complete, usually 2 to 3 hours, due to stoppages of play. Players take a warm-up before each period begins by skating around their end of the rink. Also before the start of each period you will see the *Zamboni* used to clean the ice and smooth it out to prepare it for play.

OVERTIME

One *sudden-death overtime* period of 5 minutes is played if both teams are tied at the end of regulation during *regular-season* games. It will begin after the third period ends following a two-minute rest period. Sudden-death means the first team to score a goal wins and the game ends, even if the overtime period is not completed. If both teams are still tied after one overtime period, the game ends in a tie score. The exception to this is during the *post-season* (or *playoffs*) where there can be no tied games. After a 15-minute intermission, play continues into as many overtime periods as are needed to determine a winner.

TIME-OUTS

Teams are permitted only one 30-second *time-out* per game which can only be taken when play has already stopped. Otherwise, only the *referee* can stop play, even if a player is seriously *injured*.

ATTACKING: TRYING TO SCORE GOALS

Skaters skate at about 20 miles per hour and move the puck with their sticks. When a player's stick is touching the puck and moving it, he is "in control of the puck" (he is the *puck carrier*) and it is said that his team "has the puck", or is in *possession* of the puck. He can maneuver the puck and attempt to score a goal; therefore his team is called the attacking team, or *offense*. The player with the puck has several options: he can try to *shoot* the puck for a goal if he is close enough to the net and sees a good opportunity, or he can *pass* the puck to one of his teammates.

It is legal for a player to *kick* the puck, except to score a goal. Such goals will be disallowed. Kicking is an acceptable and proper tactic for a player who has lost his stick or even if he has a stick but can't get into position fast enough to play the puck with it. A player may also direct a puck with his open hand so that he may play it with his stick. He can also catch it and drop it. However, he may not direct it with his hands into the goal or to a teammate, except in his *defensive zone*.

Figure 7: Slap shot.

Shooting

A player shoots the puck

towards an opponent's goal in an attempt to score. A player can take several different kinds of shots, depending on the situation, by propelling the puck with his stick in one of these ways:

- *Slap shot*: (See **Figure 7**) achieves an extremely high speed but is less accurate than a *wrist shot*; player raises his stick in a backswing, with his strong hand held low on the shaft and his other hand on the end as a pivot; as the stick comes down towards the puck, the player leans into the stick to put all his power behind the shot, adding velocity to the puck.

- *Wrist shot*: made with the stick blade kept on the ice; the hockey puck is propelled across the ice and towards the net by a strong flicking of the wrists; slower but more accurate than a slap shot.

- *Backhand shot*: like the wrist shot except the shot is made backhand rather than forehand.

- *Flip shot*: the puck is cupped in the stick, then flipped with the wrists off the ice up towards the goal.

Passing

Passing is when one player uses his stick to send the puck to a teammate. Passing is used to move the puck closer to the goal, to keep the puck away from the opponents or to give the puck to the player that is in the best position to score. There are several different types of passes that a player can try to use:

- *Flat pass*: a player passes the puck to a teammate along the surface of the ice.

- *Flip pass*: a player passes the puck to a teammate by lifting it with his stick into the air.

- *Drop pass*: a player simply leaves the puck behind for a teammate to pick up.

When a pass is to be sent to a teammate that is moving, the passer needs to *lead* his teammate with a *lead pass*. This means the passer will send the puck to where the moving player will be when the pass arrives.

DEFENSE: STOPPING THE TEAM WITH THE PUCK FROM SCORING

The *defense* (or defending team), the team that does not have the puck, will try to get it away from the player who controls it and prevent that team from scoring. One of the 6 players on the team is allowed to stand in front of the goal to protect it and prevent shots from going in for a score. This player is called the *goalie* and more information on him and his teammates is in the chapter on **THE TEAM & PLAYER POSITIONS**.

The other 5 players on the defending team skate around and try to get the puck away as it is being passed, block the shots headed towards the goal, or take the puck away from a player that has it on his stick. The two legal, permissible methods for stopping an opponent are *checking* and *blocking*:

- Checking: bumping into an opponent by using the stick, shoulders or hips. (See **Figure 8**) Checking is only allowed against the player in control of the puck or against the last player to control it. There are two main types of checks, *stick checks* and *body checks*. In a stick check, a player uses his stick to hook, poke or sweep the puck away from an opponent. In a body check a player bumps or slams into an opponent with either his hip or shoulder <u>only</u> to block the opponent's progress or throw him off-balance.

16

Figure 8: Checking.

- Blocking: a less common method where a player drops to one or both knees and uses his body to stop a puck; this is riskier because a smart puck carrier may be able to get around a defender that drops to his knees too soon.

Since skaters move pretty fast, there are many hard checks and physical plays. However, the players are well protected by their equipment which was described more fully in the chapter on **UNIFORMS & EQUIPMENT**.

It is when a player uses other, illegal methods to get the puck or stop his opponents that the referee will call a penalty. Penalties are discussed in great detail in the chapter entitled **PENALTIES**, and reading about those will help you recognize them.

CHOOSING SIDES FOR THE GAME

The home team starts the game defending the goal closest to its team bench. The teams then switch the goals they defend each successive period.

STARTING PLAY/ FACE-OFFS

At the beginning of each period, and to start play after it has been stopped during the game, a *face-off* is used. (See **Figure 9**) In a face-off an official drops the puck on the ice between the sticks of two opposing players, each facing his opponent's end of the ice and standing one stick-length apart. The blades of their sticks must be touching the ice. No other players may be within 15 feet of the players facing off. If either of these players is not in the proper position when the official is ready to drop the puck, the official may order a teammate of that player to take the face-off instead. This is why you may see a player who is set up for a face-off skate off unexpectedly to be replaced by a teammate in the *face-off circle*.

These two opposing players try to pass the puck to one of their teammates or shoot it toward the opponent's goal. A

Figure 9: Face-off.

face-off is a fair way to ensure that both teams have an equal chance of gaining access to the puck, although some players are better than others at winning face-offs. The *face-off spots* and *circles* are located at various places around the rink. Generally, unless the rules specify otherwise, a face-off is held near the place where the infraction occurred or where play was stopped. One exception is if the stoppage has been caused by an attacking player in his *attacking zone*, then the resulting face-off is taken back in the *neutral zone*.

STOPPING OF PLAY
There are several reasons why play may be stopped during the period:

- if a player breaks a rule and receives a penalty
- if the goalie stops a shot and holds onto the puck
- if the puck goes "out of play" or flies out of the rink
- if the referee determines a player is seriously injured
- if the *goal cage* is dislodged and moves off its spot
- if a player is injured and his team has possession of the puck
- if a player catches the puck in his hand and it is declared *dead*
- if the puck is *frozen* by two players; this means that the puck is caught between the sticks and/or skates of two opposing players and neither one of them can free it. Since the puck cannot be moved, a face-off is held to get the action started again

A GAME OF CONSTANT MOTION
In general, the puck must always be kept in motion. The team in possession of the puck can carry it behind its own goal only once and must advance it towards the opposing goal unless prevented from doing so by opposing players. A player who *freezes* the puck, holds it, or plays it along the boards in such a way to stop play will be assessed a penalty unless he is being checked by an opponent. A player outside his defensive zone may not pass or carry

the puck back into his own zone in order to stall for time, unless his team has fewer players on the ice than the opposition (called being *shorthanded*).

Formal plays in hockey are not as common as in other sports because possession of the puck is fleeting. The speed and contact allowed by the rules make it difficult for players to complete plays requiring precise timing. Therefore, rather than established plays, in ice hockey play generally follows the puck, which moves quickly all over the rink, and players must improvise actions to score.

END OF GAME SPORTSMANSHIP
At the end of every game, all the hockey players of both teams line up at opposite sides of the rink and skate toward each other so that each player on one team can shake hands with each player on the opposing team. This tradition is unique among professional sports and reminds players of the importance of good sportsmanship.

The next few sections should help you to identify the different players, reasons why play has stopped and the penalties that the officials are looking for.

THE TEAM & PLAYER POSITIONS

Each hockey team may have a maximum of 6 players on the ice at one time. The first 6 players to begin the game for a team are called the *starting lineup*. Each player has a certain job to do, and plays a certain position. The 6 positions generally played are *goalkeeper* (or *goalie*), *left defenseman*, *right defenseman*, *center*, *left wing* and *right wing*. The goalie stays near his team's goal; of the 5 players that skate around the rink, the left and right defensemen comprise the team's *defensive line*, and the center, left and right wing together make up the *forward line*. (See **Figure 10**)

Today, 20 players, including 2 goalkeepers, are a standard complete *NHL* team. A team usually will have 3 forward

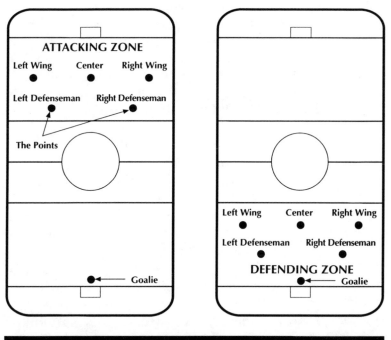

Figure 10: Player positions.

lines (9 players) and 5 or 6 defensemen to rotate in; the other 3 or 4 players are usually spare forwards or *penalty killers*.

SHORTHANDED / POWER PLAYS

When a player commits a *penalty*, his team may have to play with one less player than the other team, or *shorthanded*. The other team, which now has the advantage of outnumbering the shorthanded team, is said to be on the *power play*. These concepts are discussed in the chapter on **PENALTIES**.

SUBSTITUTIONS

Substitutions may be made at any time during play stoppages or while play is in progress, provided a team at no time has more than 6 players on the ice. Most often, substitutions are made *on-the-fly*, with substitutes skating into the game and players leaving the ice as play continues around them. The moment the player leaving the ice gets within 5 feet of the bench, his substitute can go over the *boards* and come into play. This type of substitution is why you may occasionally see a player skate right by the puck at the sideboards; if a substituting player touches the puck before the retiring player has completely left the ice, their team could be penalized for having *too many men on the ice*.

Some coaches change everyone except the goalie every 2-3 minutes to provide adequate rest. A goalie will usually play the entire game unless he gets injured or is playing very poorly. Unlike other sports where individuals are substituted for individuals, in hockey the entire *forward line* often will be replaced at once, putting players on the ice who work well together. This is called a *line change*. Scoring goals requires precision and timing which is achieved by practice and familiarity among teammates. Also, when a referee stops play because he believes a player is seriously injured, that player must be substituted for immediately, unless he is the goalie.

THE FORWARD LINE
The forward line plays nearer to the opponent's goal and is responsible for most of the scoring. It is comprised of three players: the right and left wings and a center.

Center
The center usually leads his team's attack when it is trying to score a goal. He also takes part in most of the *face-offs*. The center must be able to think and react quickly. He starts play in the center of the forward line, but the playing action can take him anywhere on the ice as he pursues the puck. Since he often possesses the puck as he and his teammates are skating toward the other team's goal, he must be able to control the puck while he is moving and be able to pass it to a teammate who is in a position to take a shot towards the goal. Good centers score many *goals* and usually have even more *assists* (as discussed in the chapter on **TEAM & INDIVIDUAL SCORING**).

Left and Right Wing
Each wing skates along the left or right side of the rink on either side of the center, approaching the goal from an angle which gives them more openings to shoot at the goal. They pass the puck to each other and to the center, trying to get the puck to the player who has the best shot at the goal. Good wings usually score more goals and fewer assists than centers. Although left and right wings cover their respective left and right sides, like the center, they can be found anywhere on the ice.

DEFENSEMEN
The *left* and *right defensemen* generally play to the rear of the team so they are available to defend their own goal. The left defenseman covers the left half of the rink, the right defenseman plays to the right, harassing the right and left wings on the other team, but they can skate into each other's territory.

Defensemen actually have a two-part job:

- When their team is defending (the opponents have the puck) the defensemen will use *checking* and *blocking* to try to steal the puck or make it impossible for the opponents to continue their attack. In the defending situation, once the puck has crossed the *blue line* into the *defensive zone*, you will see one defenseman station himself near the goal to assist his goalie, while the other defenseman will go after the player controlling the puck.

- When their team is on the attack (has the puck), they try to keep the puck in their opponent's *defensive zone* by passing it to their teammates. In this case, the defensemen are called *point men* or just *points* and they use *backchecking* (checking while skating back towards their own goal) to break up a sudden counter-attack by the defending team. They are positioned at locations called the *points*, on opposite sides of the ice just inside the attacking zone near to the opponents' blue line.

Defensemen are highly skilled at skating backwards, checking (moving their bodies against the person with the puck and making them lose control of the puck) and blocking shots at the goal. They are often the biggest, strongest members of the team. Sometimes defensemen can even lead an attack and score; a few of the NHL's most prolific scorers have been defensemen.

GOALKEEPER
He is also called the goalie, *goaltender* or *netminder*. (See **Figure 11**) The goalie generally plays the entire game unless he is injured or plays very poorly. He does not skate around the ice like his teammates; his job is to stay near his team's goal and protect it. His area is the *goal crease* in front of the goal.

Figure 11: Goalkeeper.

In playing position, the goalie's feet are just wide enough apart that his heavy leg pads are close together, with his knees slightly bent and flexible to allow him to move in either direction quickly. His body is bent forward at the waist so he can watch the puck, and he holds his stick flat on the ice in front of his skates with one hand. The other hand with the catching *glove* is ready to grab or bat at a flying puck.

The rules of hockey give the goalie certain privileges that other players do not have. He is the only player who can pick up and handle the puck or *freeze* it with his hands or body. Also, opposing players may not make deliberate contact with the goalie either inside or outside his goal crease. A shot by an attacking player that would become a goal if not *saved* by the goalie is called a *shot on goal*. The goalie tries to stop the puck (which may be traveling up to 120 miles per hour) any way he can. One of the NHL's early rules made it a $2 fine for a goalie to lie down on the ice to block a shot on goal. Today a goalie can use any means available to him to stop a shot. In addition to lying flat, he can block the shot with his gloves or his heavily padded arms and legs, he can use his stick to block or bat away a shot, or he can scoop up the puck with his special catching glove and drop it away from the goal. However, it is often wise for a goalie who is surrounded by attackers to hold onto the puck after he stops it to prevent giving the attacking team a second chance to score.

Most people think the goalie has the hardest job of all because he alone must keep the other team from scoring until his teammates are able to regain control of the puck. The goalie must have extremely fast reflexes and must be alert to the progress of the game. He and his teammates have to ensure that he can see the puck at all times, or his opponents may be able to sneak a shot past him and into the net.

PENALTY KILLERS
Certain players on a team are expert at backchecking and keeping or gaining control of a loose puck under difficult circumstances. The coach will send them in when the team is shorthanded to defend against power plays until the players in the *penalty box* serve their time and return to the game. These terms are discussed more fully in the chapter entitled **PENALTIES**.

ENFORCERS

A team may have a *policeman* or *enforcer*. He is usually the most penalized player on a team because his job is to protect his teammates from harm. The enforcer is usually a larger player who is not afraid to fight or otherwise stand up to his opponents.

Now let us see how these players and teams score *points*.

TEAM & INDIVIDUAL SCORING

The object of hockey is for one team to score more goals than the other to win the game. A legal *goal* is scored when the *puck* goes between the *goalposts* off the *stick* of an attacking player and crosses completely over the red *goal line*. A goal is not scored if the puck bounces off an *official*. The puck may not be kicked, thrown, batted by hand or deliberately directed into the net by any means other than the stick of an attacking player held below shoulder level. It is a legal score, however, if a defender accidentally bumps the puck in or if it has been deflected off of any player into the goal. No goal can be awarded if it occurs while any part of an attacking player's body is inside the *goal crease*, unless that player was pushed there by a defender. A *hat trick* is where a player scores 3 or more goals in a single game, truly an accomplishment.

When a player passes the puck to a teammate who scores, it is said he has provided assistance, or an *assist*, to the goal scorer. It is even possible for two players to pass the puck, one immediately after the other, to a third player who then scores a goal. In such a case, both players may be credited with an assist. Giving credit for assists is not as clear cut as goal scoring; it is in the discretion of the *official scorer* to decide.

When a goal is scored, the *referee* reports it to the official scorer. A few seconds later, the public will hear an announcement similar to this: "Goal scored for the Flyers, by number 10, *John LeClair*, with assists from number 88, *Eric Lindros* and number 77, *Paul Coffey*." As this example shows, assists can be credited to two players for each one goal scored, but it is not mandatory. In sum, a player can score a goal unassisted, or with the assist of one or two players.

In addition to affecting the final game score, goals and assists play a role in each player's individual scoring record. In the individual records, both an assist and a goal are worth one point. At the end of a season, a player will have accumulated a certain number of *points*, which is his total number of goals added to his total number of assists:

GOALS + ASSISTS = POINTS

A list of the career and single season record holders is in the chapter on **NHL INDIVIDUAL RECORDS**.

THE OFFICIALS

The general conduct of a hockey game is under the charge of a *referee* assisted by two *linesmen* on the ice who call infractions and hand out *penalties*. The *NHL* began using 2 referees in some games during the 1998-99 season. There are additional off-ice *officials* including two *goal judges*, a *game timekeeper*, a *penalty timekeeper*, an *official scorer*, a *statistician* with assistants and a *video goal judge*. To communicate, the on-ice officials use *hand signals* and phrases that the other officials are able to interpret to keep accurate records and convey the on-ice decisions to the fans. The hand signals for the most commonly called infractions are provided in the chapter called **OFFICIALS' HAND SIGNALS**. Keep in mind that if a *puck* strikes an official, play will continue uninterrupted because in hockey, an official is considered part of the *rink*, much like the *boards* or *goalposts*.

REFEREE
The man on skates wearing black pants and an official league sweater with red armbands is in charge and responsible for the orderly progress of the game. He carries a whistle and a tape measure. In general, the referee is responsible for starting the game, making sure the ice, nets and clock are in good condition, seeing that the other officials are present and ready for the game, and imposing penalties. He has the power to send a player to the *penalty box* and can decide that a player is *injured* seriously enough to stop play. He can retreat into an area called the *referee's crease*, located in front of the *timekeepers' table* in the rink, and no player may follow him into this area without permission or a *misconduct penalty* will be called. The referee reports goals to the scorers' bench for them to announce his decision to the fans. He must be able to see the puck at all times, or he will stop play and hold a *face-off*.

LINESMEN

Two other men on skates, one toward each end of the rink, wearing black pants and an official league sweater (but without red armbands) assist the referee; they also carry whistles. These *linesmen* call *offsides*, *icing*, play stoppages and handle face-offs. They are also responsible for breaking up any fights, allowing the referee to watch the action and decide which penalties to call. Linesmen call *minor penalties* that they observe in addition to drawing the referee's attention to infractions he may not have seen. The linesmen also retrieve the puck when play is stopped.

GOAL JUDGES

One person behind each goal will decide when a puck has crossed the goal line and will switch on a red light that signals a goal has been scored. These two people are stationed in two separate protected areas behind the opposite *endboards*, positioned so they can easily see the play and puck near the goals. Their decisions are simple: either a goal has been scored or not. The referee can overrule the goal judge's decision and disallow a goal.

GAME TIMEKEEPER

One person controls the official timing device during the three 20-minute *periods* and any *overtime* that is played. The game timekeeper watches the master clock and signals the end of each period, records the time at which the game and each of the periods starts and ends, stops the clock every time the whistle blows, starts it again when the puck is dropped in a face-off, sounds the device which indicates the end of the period and instructs the public address announcer to inform all present when there is only one minute left to play in a period.

PENALTY TIMEKEEPER

Another timekeeper assists the game timekeeper by keeping track of every player sent to the penalty box and their respective sentences to ensure offenders serve the required time for their penalties. In general, the penalty timekeeper keeps records of all penalties, of time served, and of any *penalty shots* taken on the ice, including the names of the shooters and the results of the shots.

OFFICIAL SCORER

The official scorer maintains a written record on a special form of the number of goals, the player scoring each goal, the player(s) credited with an *assist*, the time at which each goal was scored, the total number of shots, the number of *saves* by each goalie and the penalties. Although it is the referee who designates the player to be credited with a goal, it is the scorer who decides who to credit with the assists. As such, he is located in a place where he has full view of the rink, and he also communicates with the public-address announcer so his decisions can be announced to the fans.

STATISTICIAN

One individual, with as many assistants as are needed, must correctly record for the official NHL records all the actions of all of the other officials, the players and both teams. Once the referee signs these records they become official, and copies are sent to each team and to the league office after each game.

VIDEO GOAL JUDGE

Certain situations involving the puck in and around the goal area and the clock are subject to review by a *video goal judge*. These include disputes on whether the puck actually crossed the goal line, how it was directed into the goal, how much time remained on the clock when a goal was scored, and whether or not the net was dislodged before the score. The video goal judge also determines if an attacking player was in the *goal crease* when the puck crossed the *goal line*. Before 1998, a referee had to request such a ruling, but a new rule allows the video goal judge to tell the referee about a violation without being asked.

PENALTIES

In hockey there are *team penalties* and *individual penalties* called by the *officials* when a player or players break rules. A team penalty generally results in a *face-off*. There are 6 categories of individual penalties: *minor, major, bench, match* (game), *misconduct* and the *penalty shot*, each of which is treated differently. A player who commits an individual infraction spends actual game time off the ice.

Only a *captain* or alternate captain can question or discuss with the *referee* anything concerning the rules; any other player who does so will be penalized. No player, including the captain, may protest a call or he will be penalized for misconduct. The rules simply do not permit any players to complain about penalties.

Oftentimes, penalties for actions meant to intentionally cause serious harm are also punishable by multiple-game suspensions and monetary fines imposed by the *NHL*. Such fines and suspensions are not discussed in great detail here, but can make for interesting news when they occur.

TEAM PENALTIES
These are the most common violations and they result only in a face-off.

Offsides
The purpose of the *offsides* rule is to prevent an attacking player from waiting in front of the opponent's goal for a long pass from a teammate, giving him an easier chance to score. To prevent this, the rule requires that the attacking players must all follow the puck into the attacking zone; they may not go in ahead of the puck. An attacking player is considered offsides if both his skates go over the *blue line* into the attacking zone before the puck does. (See **Figure 12**) If only one skate is over the blue line, with the player

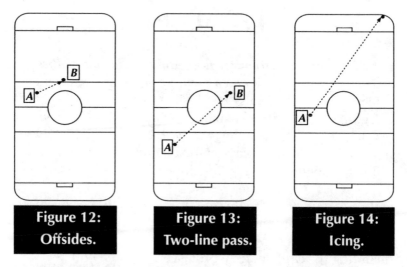

| Figure 12: | Figure 13: | Figure 14: |
| Offsides. | Two-line pass. | Icing. |

straddling the line, he is *onsides* and there is no infraction. That is why you may sometimes see players skating strangely near the blue line. A face-off is held outside the attacking zone near the spot where the offside violation occurred.

An official may call a *delayed offsides* by raising his arm but not blowing his whistle until he sees the outcome of the play. He may wait to call the penalty because if the defense is able to quickly get control of the puck, stopping the play would penalize the non-offending team by stopping its momentum. In this case, the offsides is waved off, or cancelled, by the official and play continues uninterrupted.

Two-line Pass
The *two-line pass* is another type of offsides violation. A two-line pass violation occurs when a pass is received by a teammate after the puck passes over one of the blue lines and the red *center line* without being touched. (See **Figure 13**) However, like a regular offsides it is no penalty if the puck precedes the player across the center line. A face-off is held near the spot where the two-line pass violation occurred.

Icing

The *icing* infraction occurs when the team in possession of the puck shoots toward the goal from behind the red center line, the puck goes into the end of the rink across the red *goal line* (but not into the goal) and a member of the opposing team touches the puck first. (See **Figure 14**) A face-off is then held in the penalized team's defensive zone. It is not icing if the puck happens to go in the goal. In the NHL, icing is never called against a team that is playing *shorthanded*, if the puck is touched by the goalie before it crosses the goal line, if the puck passes through any part of the *goal crease* before it crosses the goal line or if a member of the attacking team touches it first. Additionally, an official who determines that a defender could have easily stopped the puck before it crossed the goal line may decide not to call icing.

Icing sometimes may be a good strategy for a team's players. It may provide them a break in the action, allowing for rest and substitutions, or may give them a chance to plan or change tactics, especially when the opponents are about to score.

Other Penalties

The referee may stop play and call a face-off for certain infractions he deems unintentional and not directed against another player. Two such plays are batting the puck with a *high stick* or briefly *carrying the puck* with the hand. Intentional infractions of these rules are discussed below under Individual Penalties.

INDIVIDUAL PENALTIES & SHORTHANDED PLAY

Violations of certain rules punish the offending player by removing him from the action of the game and requiring him to serve actual playing time sitting on the *penalty bench* in the *penalty box* while his team plays with one less man. The penalized team will play with one less player than the other team, or *shorthanded*, unless the other team also has a player removed by a penalty. Most individual penalties are called because a player illegally interfered with an opponent, deliberately tried to hurt another player or played in a dangerous manner. Whenever a penalty is called, play stops, the penalized player leaves the ice and a face-off is used to restart the action. This face-off is usually held near the location where the infraction occurred.

A team may also have to play with only 4 players (2 men short) if a second penalty is called against a player on the same team before the penalty against the first player expires. There is no limit to the number of penalties that can be called against a team. However, no matter how many penalties are called against a team, that team never plays with less than 4 men on the ice at a time (including one goalie).

Penalties that would cause a team to play with less than 4 men become *delayed penalties* and are served only as the time on prior penalties expires. Delayed penalties are then served in the order they were committed. When a third player is penalized after two of his teammates are already in the penalty box, he joins them in the penalty box but a substitute goes out to replace the third player on the ice. Even though his team still has the same number of players on the ice, this third penalty hurts his team in another way. When the first penalized player's penalty time expires, he must go directly to the bench instead of back onto the ice. He can then only re-enter as a substitute.

The 6 types of individual penalties and the penalty imposed for each are discussed on the following pages. Goalie penalties are treated separately. Each type of penalty is punishable by a specific length of time served in the penalty box. Note that any penalty time remaining at the end of a period will carry over and be served at the start of the next period.

Minor Penalties

A player who commits a minor infraction will spend 2 minutes in the penalty box. If his opponents score while he is in the penalty box and his team is shorthanded, the penalized player may return to the ice immediately. The most common minor penalties are those which endanger an opponent or impede his progress; less common are those called for equipment violations. The category of offenses includes *interference, tripping, boarding, cross-checking, slashing, charging, elbowing, holding, high-sticking, hooking,* closing the hand on the puck, playing with a broken stick, deliberately *falling on the puck,* holding the puck against the boards when not being checked, *leaving the bench illegally* and *roughing.* A new rule imposes a penalty on any player who fakes an action or takes a *dive* trying to draw a penalty call on the opposing team.

Double minors (lasting 4 minutes) are assessed in one of two cases:
- for an accidental infraction that resulted in injury
- for an attempt to injure a player without actual injury resulting

These are called for infractions that are between a minor and major penalty in seriousness. If the opposing team scores a goal while a player is serving a double minor, only one 2-minute penalty is subtracted from the time he must serve.

Major Penalties

These are assessed for many of the same infractions that apply to minor penalties, where the referee judges that either a greater degree of violence, or deliberate violence was used against an opponent. When a minor penalty is committed but blood is drawn, it <u>automatically</u> becomes a major penalty. The penalized player spends 5 minutes in the penalty box and there is no premature return to the ice even if a goal is scored. *Fighting* and *spearing* are two infractions always calling for major penalties. If the same player is cited three times in one game for a major penalty, he must leave the game and not return. In all cases, a substitute may come on the ice for this penalized player after 5 minutes.

Bench Penalties

This type of penalty is called whenever anybody on the *bench* commits an infraction such as using improper language with an official, throwing something on the ice, improperly leaving the bench, or in any way interfering with the game or an official. It may also be assessed for an infraction relating to an improper change to the *starting lineup,* or for illegal substitutions, such as having *too many men on the ice.* One of the players on the ice, other than the goalie, must spend 2 minutes in the penalty box. The coach of the penalized team designates to the referee which player will serve time.

Game or Match Penalties

Such penalties are rare, and are the most serious, calling for banishment from the game and a monetary fine. A player who deliberately injures another player must leave the game for its duration and be replaced by a substitute who must serve 5 minutes in the penalty box. During this time, the penalized player's team must play shorthanded. The third major penalty called on the same player during one game also results in his being ruled off the ice for the balance of the game.

Misconduct Penalties

Misconduct penalties differ from all others in that they permit immediate substitution, and the penalized player's team does not play shorthanded. Banishment is generally for 10 minutes following the use of abusive language or gestures, *unsportsmanlike conduct,* the failure to follow an official's orders, gesturing disrespectfully to any person, showing disrespect for a ruling, knocking or shooting the puck out of the reach of an official who is retrieving it, throwing equipment into the playing area, banging the boards with the sticks, not proceeding directly to the penalty box when instructed to do so or ignoring a warning to stop trying to incite an opponent into incurring a penalty.

Serious misconduct or abuse of an official can result in a *game misconduct*, where a penalized player is banished for the rest of the game. A rule instituted to reduce fighting, the *third-man-in rule* states that the third player involved in a fight will be assessed a game misconduct, even if he was only trying to break the fight up.

Penalty Shot

Although it is rarely called, the *penalty shot* is one of the most exciting plays in hockey. An attacking player is allowed to maneuver the puck from center ice in alone on the goalie in an attempt to score while all the other players are stationed behind the red center line. The puck is placed in the *center face-off circle*, and the player can stickhandle it anywhere to set up his shot. Once he crosses the attacking blue line, however, he must continue forward toward the goal. Only one shot at the goal is allowed and a rebound shot does not count.

A penalty shot is usually awarded when a player is illegally prevented from a clear scoring opportunity, such as when he is illegally interfered with from behind as he is moving in on the goal unopposed, or when a defending player other than the goalie picks up or deliberately falls on the puck while it is in his own goal crease. It is generally the player who was fouled who must take the penalty shot, though in some instances the captain of the non-offending team has to select a player on the ice to take the shot. In the past, the shooter of a penalty shot had the advantage, but today's goalies are able to stop the majority of these attempts. In fact, if the player taking the penalty shot is not accustomed to stickhandling or to shooting the puck, the penalized team may prefer the penalty shot to playing 2 minutes shorthanded.

Goalie Penalties

The *goalie* will generally remain in the game even if he commits a minor or major penalty infraction. One of his teammates who is on the ice at the time of the infraction will go to the penalty box and serve the goalie's time. This player is designated by the coach or manager of the offending team. However, a goalie who commits 3 major penalties will get a game misconduct penalty and must leave the game like any other player. Likewise, a goalie who commits a match penalty must also leave the game. In both cases, a substitute replaces the goalie. If a goalie holds onto a puck when there are no opposing players around to check him, or if he intentionally bats the puck out of the rink with his stick, he will be called for a minor penalty called *delay of game*.

Coincidental Penalties

Coincidental penalties occur when an equal number of players on opposing teams receive major or minor penalties of equal length at the same time. When only one minor penalty is called on each team, the players serve their time without substitution like a normal minor penalty. However, when coincidental penalties are called on more than one player on each team, or there are players already in the penalty box from either team, the penalties have the effect of cancelling each other out. Although these penalized players serve their time in the penalty box, substitutes immediately replace them on the ice. This is to prevent coincidental penalties from causing teams to skate with fewer than 5 players. Once their penalty time has expired, the penalized players can return to the ice only after play has stopped for some other reason, to allow the substitute players to leave the ice.

Delayed Penalties

You might wonder why some penalties are called immediately by the referee while others are delayed. When a team in *possession* of the puck commits a penalty, the whistle is blown and play is stopped immediately. But when a player on the team not controlling the puck commits an infraction, the referee will point to the offending player but will wait until the team in possession of the puck completes its play either with a goal or a loss of possession before blowing his whistle and stopping play. The purpose of this delay is simply to allow a non-offending team in possession of the puck a chance to score a goal, if it can, without interruption. If the penalty is a minor, and the non-offending team scores a goal, the penalty will not be imposed on the offending team. Major penalties are imposed regardless of whether a goal is scored.

Power Plays

When a team plays with all 6 players on the ice, it is at *full strength*. When a team has fewer players on the ice than its opponent due to penalties, this is called playing *shorthanded*. When one team plays shorthanded, the other team enjoys a *power play*, one of the few set plays in hockey and one of the most exciting. In a power play, the team with more players on the ice tries to position all its players except the goalie near the opponent's goal. From this location they will take shot after shot at the goal, trying to overwhelm the opponent's goalie. The shorthanded team tries to *kill the penalty* (prevent their opponent from scoring until they are back at full strength). To respond to the power play, the shorthanded team sends in substitute players called *penalty killers*, who are expert at getting the puck away from the opponents, keeping it away by excellent stickhandling or helping the goalie defend the goal.

Some trivia: It used to be that a team stayed shorthanded the full 2 minutes of a minor penalty, but the *Montreal*

Canadiens of the 1950s were so strong on the power play that they could score 2, 3 or as many as 4 goals during the 2 minutes. The rule used in the NHL today, where a penalized player returns to the ice as soon as <u>one goal</u> is scored, was changed to prevent such unbalanced scoring.

<u>Common Individual Penalties</u>
Below are described some of the most common offenses for which penalties are assessed against players. Officials use different hand signals to communicate each of these, shown with a description in the chapter entitled **OFFICIALS' HAND SIGNALS**.

- Boarding: when a player violently thrusts an opponent into the boards by body checking, elbowing or tripping

- Charging: a deliberate move of more than two steps to run into an opponent. Also, jumping into an opponent to check him. Note: there is a slight difference between *legal* checking and *illegal* charging; only a player with the puck, or who just gave up the puck, can be checked, and officials will count the number of strides a player takes before he makes contact with an opponent he is checking. If more than 2 steps are taken and a player gets up too much speed/force before hitting his opponent, it is charging.

- Cross-checking: when a player *stick checks* an opponent with both hands on the stick and no part of the stick on the ice (See **Figure 15**)

- Delay of game: imposed on a player or goalkeeper who purposely delays the game in any way, such as by shooting or batting the puck outside the playing area to stall for time or displacing the goalpost from its normal position as an opponent is coming in for a shot

- Elbowing: when a player strikes an opponent with his elbow

Figure 15: Cross-checking.

- Falling on the puck: when a player falls on the puck, gathers it close to his body or closes his hand around it. Note that a player can knock the puck down with his glove, but he cannot slap it or push it deliberately to a teammate unless he is in his defensive zone. This is called a *hand pass* and results in a face-off.

- Fighting: fisticuffs between players. If the referee deems that one player instigated the fight, that player receives an additional minor, misconduct or game misconduct penalty. A player who removes his jersey before a fight automatically receives a game misconduct.

- High-Sticking: when a player checks an opponent with his stick above the height of his opponent's shoulders

- Holding: when one player holds onto or wraps his arms around an opponent or the opponent's stick to impede his progress

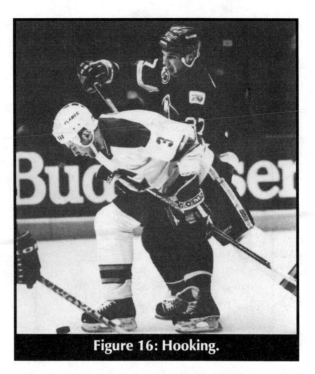

Figure 16: Hooking.

- Hooking: when a player attempts to impede the progress of another player by hooking him with the blade of his stick (See **Figure 16**)

- Interference: when a player attempts to impede the motion of another player not in possession of the puck. In recent years, the NHL has urged officials to be more aggressive in enforcing this rule because skating free of obstructions is essential to the speed and fluidity of the game and its most skilled players.

- Kneeing: when a player strikes an opponent with his knee

- Roughing: when a player shoves or is involved in a minor altercation or scuffle; a less severe form of fighting

Figure 17: Spearing.

- Slashing: when a player swings his stick in a slashing motion at an opponent

- Spearing: when a player thrusts his stick at an opponent in a bayonet fashion (See **Figure 17**)

- Too many men on the ice: can occur during substitution, if a substituting player touches the puck or makes any physical contact with an opposing player before a retiring teammate has completely left the ice

- Tripping: when a player trips an opponent with his stick or part of his body

Now that you have learned the basics of ice hockey, it is time to explore some of the finer points of hockey strategy.

THINGS TO LOOK FOR DURING PLAY / STRATEGY

Hockey is a sport which can be difficult to understand because of its fast action and unique rules. However, with some basic knowledge of what to look for, you will be able to enjoy the strategy and hard-hitting action of this great sport.

WATCHING THE PUCK
Look for *caroms* or rebounds of the *puck*. In hockey, the puck often ricochets off the *boards* after hard shots or passes. In fact, hockey players use the boards like billiards players use the bumpers of a pool table. Therefore, when a player shoots the puck hard at one of the boards, look for the puck to be where a bounce off the boards would take it.

MATCH-UPS
A *match-up* is defined as a pairing of players on opposing teams who will *cover* each other during the hockey game. To cover a player is to stay close to prevent him from receiving a pass or making a play on offense. These pairings are vital, and coaches are always trying to get the edge on the other team by exploiting a player's known weaknesses. An *NHL* rule requires the visiting team to name its *starting lineup* first to give the home team an advantage, allowing it to respond with the players and *forward* and *defensive lines* it feels are best suited to handle the visitors' lineup. The *referee* must always allow the home team the option of making the final change of players, not only at the start of a *period*, but prior to any *face-off*, as well. That is why you will often see referees order certain players off the ice before a face-off, ruling that the visiting team may not make any more changes.

ATTACK PATTERNS
In hockey, players can quickly skate from one end of the *rink* to another. Therefore, when a player has control of the

puck, he can quickly develop a chance to score a *goal* by skating toward the opponent's goal with his teammates. This is called a *break* or *rush*, and often catches the defense off-guard with little time to skate backwards into position.

Situations develop where the number of players on the attacking team (*offense*) may outnumber the opponents in the *attacking zone*. For example, if 2 attackers are defended by only 1 defenseman (in addition to the goalie) on a break, this is called a *2-on-1 break*. There are also *2-on-2* and *3-on-1* breaks. The more outnumbered the defenders are, the greater the chance is that the attacking team will have a man *open* for a *shot on goal*. An open player is one that is not covered by any defenders.

The extreme example of the break is the *breakaway*, where an attacker with the puck skates undefended towards the goal. This situation is similar to a penalty shot in that it pits a sole attacker against the goaltender in a one-on-one showdown.

ATTACK STRATEGIES
The attacking team will often try the following strategies to improve its chances of scoring:

Dumping The Puck Into The Zone
Because of the *offsides* rule, attacking players must be careful to stay out of the attacking zone until the puck has crossed the *blue line*. When one or more players from the attacking team are about to commit an offsides by crossing the blue line ahead of the puck, their teammate with the puck will often *dump* or shoot the puck into the attacking zone, where they chase after it and hope to regain control. In an example shown in **Figure 18**, player A dumps the puck so teammates B and C can enter the *attacking zone* without being offsides.

Deking
In hockey, *deking* is an art used by the *puck carrier* to make a

defending player think the puck carrier is going to pass or move in a certain direction when he is not. Body control and stickhandling are the keys to successful deking. A player's chest usually gives his true intentions away and a good defender watches this and *body checks* his opponent here. There are three main types of dekes:

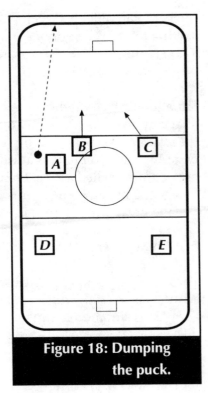

Figure 18: Dumping the puck.

- *Shoulder deke*: a quick move of the shoulder in one direction and the player in another.

- *Head deke*: a player drops his head as though moving one way and quickly moves in another.

- *Stick deke*: the stick is moved as though for a shot, but instead the player moves the puck past the defending player.

Where To Shoot The Puck In The Net

Players usually try to shoot the puck towards areas of the net that are most difficult for the *goaltender* to defend. The five most popular locations that players aim for are the upper and lower left and right corners of the goal and between the goalie's legs, called the *five-hole*. (See **Figure 19**) Because a goalie is slower with his feet than with his hands, it is usually more effective to shoot in the lower corners where he can only use his feet and stick to stop shots. Shots towards the upper corners are often more easily fended off or caught by the goalie's quicker hands.

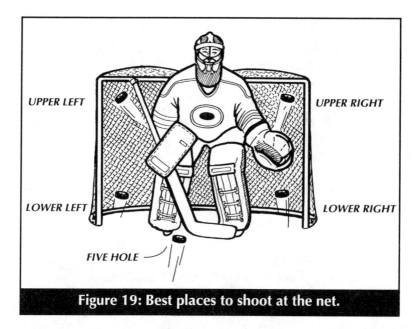

UPPER LEFT

UPPER RIGHT

LOWER LEFT

LOWER RIGHT

FIVE HOLE

Figure 19: Best places to shoot at the net.

These higher shots should be taken when the goalie is on his knees or lying on the ice and less able to defend the upper part of the goal.

Screening The Goalie
Goalies have extremely quick reactions, able to stop shots they can see clearly from fairly short range. Therefore, players from the attacking team often try to stand in front of the goalie (although legally they must stay outside the *goal crease*) to partially block or *screen* his view. If the goalie cannot see the puck coming until the last instant, he has less time to react and make a *save*.

Deflections
The same players who screen the goalie are also in excellent position to *deflect* with their sticks a shot or a pass into the net. A goalie anticipates the puck's flight from seeing the direction it takes off the shooter's stick, and often cannot react in time to stop a *deflection* that changes the puck's direction.

DEFENSE STRATEGY
Defending players try to stop attacking players any way they can. Defenders try to knock the puck away or physically disrupt the puck carrier so that he loses control of the puck and his momentum. Good defenders do this with nimble skating, skillful use of the hockey stick and hard *checking*.

Playing The Man / Checking
Rather than just trying to knock the puck away with their sticks, a much safer strategy for players on the defending team is to cover the player, checking him often and making sure he cannot get off a good pass or shot. Going just for the puck is riskier because if the defender misses the puck, the attacking player may get around the defender and have an open pass or shot on goal.

GOALIE STRATEGY: CUTTING DOWN THE ANGLE
When an attacker skates towards the goal with the puck, the goalie will often come out of the goal several feet to *cut down the angle* of the attacker's shot, leaving him with less *net* area to shoot at by making himself closer and larger to the shooter. (See **Figure 20**) However, this is risky because if an attacker gets the puck past the goalie, he has an open shot at the net.

POWER PLAYS
A *power play* is a critical juncture in a hockey game because it is an excellent scoring opportunity for the team with the extra player(s). This situation calls for some different strategies than the rest of the game when the teams are both at equal strength.

Power Play Set Up
The team that has an extra man or men (the team on the power play) tries to get set up in the attacking zone. Since it outnumbers the *shorthanded* team on the ice, it will always have at least one man that is open, or not defended.

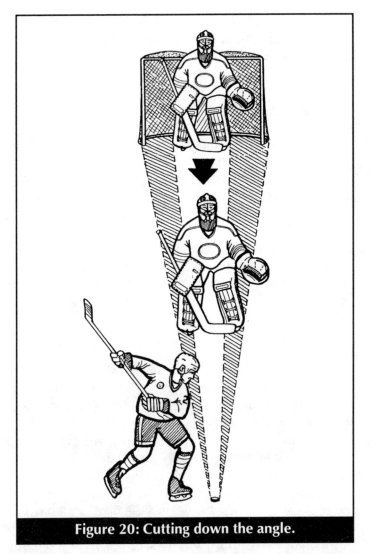

Figure 20: Cutting down the angle.

The best way for it to capitalize on this advantage is if all of its players are positioned in the attacking zone where each can pass and take shots at the goal. After setting up, players on the power play pass the puck around quickly to try to find the player with the best open shot. The two defensemen of that team set up at the *points* from which they can shoot at the net or pass to their teammates. The players at the points also help prevent the puck from leaving the zone. If the puck does leave the zone, to prevent an offsides call, all the attacking players must *clear the zone*, or leave the attacking zone, before the puck can be brought back in.

<u>Shorthanded Strategy</u>
The team that has fewer players than the opposition, or the *shorthanded* team, tries to hold off the relentless attack of the opposition. It tries to regain control of the puck and keep it away from the team on the power play, allowing time on the penalty to wind down and expire, which is called *killing the penalty*. When the opposition is set up in its attacking zone, the shorthanded team always tries to *clear the puck*, or shoot it out of its *defensive zone*, causing the opposition to restart its power play set up all over again. A shorthanded team cannot be called for *icing*, so its players will not hesitate to slap the puck out of their own zone as hard as they can.

PULLING THE GOALIE
When a team is losing by only a few goals near the end of a game and needs to score desperately, it will often remove or *pull the goalie* from the game and replace him with a skating player who can help with the attack. This other player has none of the privileges of the goalie; for example, he cannot handle the puck freely and is not protected from contact. This desperation tactic is used by a team to get more scoring power on the ice in the final minutes of the game so it can catch up, but leaves the team's own net unguarded by a goalie. Such a wide-open net may leave the other team an opportunity to score easily if it regains possession of the puck. This type of goal is called an *empty-net goal*.

NHL TEAMS, DIVISIONS
and CONFERENCES

LEAGUE HISTORY

The *NHL* began in 1917 with 6 Canadian teams. It has changed in size many times over the years with the addition of teams (called *expansion*) or as teams ceased operations and were dissolved. In 1942-43, only 6 teams were active and they made up the NHL for the next 24 years. These teams were:

Boston Bruins	*Montreal Canadiens*
Chicago Blackhawks	New York Rangers
Detroit Red Wings	Toronto Maple Leafs

The 1967 expansion added 6 teams bringing the total to 12, divided into the East and West divisions. Six more teams were added over the next 7 years, and in 1974 the NHL was reorganized into the Prince of Wales and Clarence Campbell Conferences. It was not until 1973-74 that an expansion team (which means a team other than one of the 6 listed above), the Philadelphia Flyers, won a Stanley Cup. Four more teams were absorbed into the league in 1979 when the defunct *World Hockey Association* merged with the NHL, bringing the total to 21.

The next wave of expansion did not come until the 1990s when 5 more teams were added to the NHL, establishing professional hockey for the first time in areas of the Southeastern and Western U.S. Teams began playing in Anaheim, California (Mighty Ducks), Florida (Panthers), Tampa (Lightning), San Jose (Sharks), and Ottawa (Senators). As part of this expansion, in 1993 the names of the NHL's *divisions* and *conferences* were changed to more accurately reflect the geographic regions represented by teams. The *Wales Conference* became the *Eastern Conference*, the *Campbell Conference* became the *Western Conference*, and the names of each division was changed (e.g. the *Patrick Division* became the Northeast Division).

EXPANSION

The late 1990s and the early 21st Century is bringing further growth to the NHL. Between the 1998-99 and 2000-01 seasons, 4 new *expansion teams* are being added, bringing the total number to 30 teams. The expansion schedule is as follows:

Season Entering NHL	Team
1998-1999	Nashville
1999-2000	Atlanta
2000-2001	Columbus, Ohio
2000-2001	Minneapolis-St. Paul

To manage this growth, beginning with the 1998-99 season the NHL has added 2 more divisions for a total of six 5-team divisions in 2 conferences as shown below:

Eastern Conference
• Atlantic Division
• Northeast Division
• Southeast Division

Western Conference
• Central Division
• Northwest Division
• Pacific Division

An example of how NHL teams are listed in the newspaper by division and conference is located in the chapter entitled **DECIPHERING HOCKEY STATISTICS IN THE NEWSPAPER**.

Shown in **Table 1** is an alphabetized list of the 30 NHL teams, the year they joined the NHL, and their divisions and conferences:

TABLE 1: NHL TEAMS

Team	Year	Pre-1993 Division	Pre-1993 Conference	Realigned Division	Realigned Conference
Anaheim Mighty Ducks	1993	————	————	Pacific	Western
Atlanta Thrashers	1999			Southeast	Eastern
Boston Bruins	1924	Adams	Wales	Northeast	Eastern
Buffalo Sabres	1970	Adams	Wales	Northeast	Eastern
Calgary Flames[1]	1972	Smythe	Campbell	Northwest	Western
Carolina Hurricanes[2,3]	1979	Adams	Wales	Southeast	Eastern
Chicago Blackhawks	1926	Norris	Campbell	Central	Western
Colorado Avalanche[3,4]	1979	Adams	Wales	Northwest	Western
Columbus Blue Jackets	2000	————	————	Central	Western
Dallas Stars[5]	1967	Norris	Campbell	Pacific	Western
Detroit Red Wings	1926	Norris	Campbell	Central	Western
Edmonton Oilers[3]	1979	Smythe	Campbell	Northwest	Western
Florida Panthers	1993	————	————	Southeast	Eastern
Los Angeles Kings	1967	Smythe	Campbell	Pacific	Western
Minnesota Wild	2000			Northwest	Western
Montreal Canadiens	1917	Adams	Wales	Northeast	Eastern
Nashville Predators	1998	————	————	Central	Western
New Jersey Devils[6]	1974	Patrick	Wales	Atlantic	Eastern
New York Islanders	1972	Patrick	Wales	Atlantic	Eastern
New York Rangers	1926	Patrick	Wales	Atlantic	Eastern
Ottawa Senators	1992	Adams	Wales	Northeast	Eastern
Philadelphia Flyers	1967	Patrick	Wales	Atlantic	Eastern
Phoenix Coyotes[3,7]	1979	Smythe	Campbell	Central	Western
Pittsburgh Penguins	1967	Patrick	Wales	Atlantic	Eastern
San Jose Sharks	1991	Smythe	Campbell	Pacific	Western
St. Louis Blues	1967	Norris	Campbell	Central	Western
Tampa Bay Lightning	1992	Norris	Campbell	Southeast	Eastern
Toronto Maple Leafs	1917	Norris	Campbell	Northeast	Eastern
Vancouver Canucks	1970	Smythe	Campbell	Northwest	Western
Washington Capitals	1974	Patrick	Wales	Southeast	Eastern

[1] transferred from Atlanta in 1980
[2] were the Hartford Whalers until 1997
[3] began in the *WHA* in 1972 and were absorbed into the NHL through the 1979 merger
[4] were the Quebec Nordiques until 1995
[5] were the Minnesota North Stars until 1993
[6] originated in Kansas City; were the Colorado Rockies 1976-82
[7] were the Winnipeg Jets until 1996

NHL SEASON,
PLAYOFFS and
THE STANLEY CUP

REGULAR SEASON
The *regular season* for *NHL* hockey is 82 games long. A season is referred to as the 1998-99 season, for example, because it starts the first week in October in one year and ends in mid-April of the following calendar year. A team usually plays half of its games at home and half on the road.

During regular-season play, NHL teams compete for the top spots in the *standings*. Teams are ranked within each *division* based on a simple *point* system:
- A team receives 2 points for each game it wins
- A team receives 1 point for each game that ends in a tie
- Zero points are awarded for losses

The more points a team has, the higher it is ranked; first place is the highest position (*division leader*), followed by second place, etc. Teams can be tied for a ranking. A team's record will be described by three numbers at any given point during a season, denoting *wins-losses-ties* (for example 40-15-4). The total of these three numbers is the number of games a team has played thus far in the season; in our example it would be 59 games.

PLAYOFFS
After the regular-season schedule of games is over, 16 teams will advance to the *post-season*, otherwise known as the *Stanley Cup Playoffs*. The schedules for the playoffs will vary each year depending on how long each *round* lasts, but generally the playoffs begin in late-April and end in early-June. When there were fewer teams in the NHL

some critics complained that too many teams were rewarded with playoff berths which made the regular season less meaningful. As the NHL continues to expand, this criticism should decrease.

The top 8 teams in each of the 2 conferences make the playoffs. There are 4 rounds of playoffs used to narrow the number of teams by eliminating the losers of each round. Teams are paired up to play a *best-of-seven series* in each of the rounds. A best-of-seven game format means the first team to win 4 games emerges victorious. This can be done in as few as 4 games or in 5, 6 or 7 games. Over a seven-game series there is less chance that a weaker team can get lucky and advance to the next round than if only a single game were played.

With the NHL *realignment* into 6 divisions starting with the 1998-99 season, the method of choosing teams for the playoffs changed. The 3 division champions in each conference now automatically qualify for the playoffs and are seeded #1 through #3 according to their regular season record. The teams with the next 5 best records in each conference also qualify and are seeded #4 through #8.

In the First Round the #1 team from each conference plays against the #8 team, #2 vs. #7, #3 vs. #6, and #4 vs. #5. A total of eight First Round series will be played, four in each conference. The winners of these First Round series then play each other in the Second Round, called the Conference Semifinals, as shown in the diagram of playoff brackets. (See **Figure 21**) The Third Round is the Conference Finals that determines the champion of each conference. To honor the builders of hockey, the winners of the Eastern Conference receive the Prince of Wales Trophy and the winners of the Western Conference receive the Campbell Bowl as rewards for their victories.

These two conference champions will then meet for the final, or fourth, round which is called the *Stanley Cup*

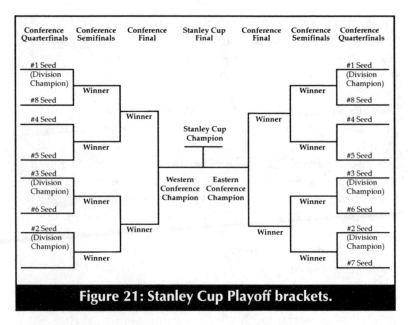

| Conference Quarterfinals | Conference Semifinals | Conference Final | Stanley Cup Final | Conference Final | Conference Semifinals | Conference Quarterfinals |

#1 Seed (Division Champion)
#8 Seed
Winner
Winner
#4 Seed
#5 Seed
Winner

Stanley Cup Champion

Western Conference Champion   Eastern Conference Champion

#3 Seed (Division Champion)
#6 Seed
Winner
#2 Seed (Division Champion)
Winner
Winner

#1 Seed (Division Champion)
#8 Seed
Winner
#4 Seed
#5 Seed
Winner
#3 Seed (Division Champion)
#6 Seed
Winner
#2 Seed (Division Champion)
#7 Seed
Winner

Figure 21: Stanley Cup Playoff brackets.

Finals, to determine the best team in the NHL. The winners of the Stanley Cup Finals are awarded the highly-coveted *Stanley Cup*, a silver trophy that stands 3 feet high, engraved with the names of each member of every Stanley Cup championship team. (See **Figure 22**) It is the oldest trophy competed for by professional athletes in North America. The Stanley Cup is held by one team until a new champion claims it. Although there can be a new champion every year, some teams have established dynasties, reclaiming the Cup several years in succession, such as the *Montreal Canadiens*, the Edmonton Oilers, the Toronto Maple Leafs and the New York Islanders.

HISTORY OF THE STANLEY CUP

In 1893, Canada's Governor-General, Sir Frederick Arthur, also known as Lord Stanley of Preston, bought a large trophy to give to an amateur hockey club in Montreal. He used his own pocket money to buy the silver cup, spending 10 pounds (or about $50 in American money). He placed this cup in the hands of a board of trustees to award it to the amateur hockey champions of Canada each year. However, as the sport of hockey grew in popularity, semi-pro and then professional teams were formed, and the trustees decided to make the cup an international hockey prize. Unfortunately for Lord Stanley, his term of office expired in May 1893, and he returned to England 10 months before the first playoffs having never seen a single Stanley Cup game.

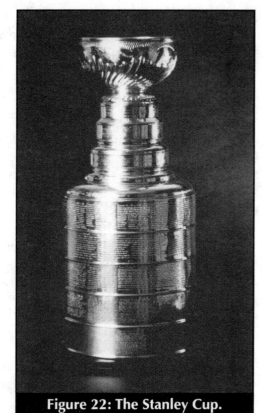

Figure 22: The Stanley Cup.

Winners of the Stanley Cup receive the trophy right on the ice after their final victory, and one player skates around the rink holding the Cup above his head. Despite its status, the Stanley Cup has had to be retrieved from assorted unusual locations: it has been thrown in a river, tossed over a graveyard fence, used as a flowerpot by an unsuspecting housewife, forgotten on the side of the road after the changing of a flat tire, and even stolen from the Chicago Stadium showcase by a Montreal fan who felt it belonged back in Montreal.

Although that fan was mistaken, the city of Montreal is indeed rich in Stanley Cup tradition. The first Stanley Cup match was held there on March 22, 1894 with the Montreal AAA's defeating the Ottawa Capitals by a score of 3-1.

Also the Montreal Canadiens have won the cup 24 times since 1923, an incredible record of domination that is not likely to be broken anytime soon. The teams with the next-most Stanley Cup titles to their names are the Toronto Maple Leafs with 13 and the Detroit Red Wings with 9.

Some of the most memorable Stanley Cup series include the 1919 championship which ended with no decision because of a flu epidemic; the longest game in hockey history was played in the 1936 series, a scoreless game that lasted 176 minutes and 30 seconds into the 6th overtime before the winning goal was scored; the 1942 series in which Detroit, despite having won the first 3 games, lost the next 4 in a row and the series to Toronto; the 1951 series in which every one of the 5 games it took for Toronto to beat Montreal went into overtime; and the 1980 series in which the New York Islanders won 6 of 7 overtime games to defeat the Philadelphia Flyers, the first of the team's 4 consecutive Stanley Cup victories.

The Stanley Cup has been won by the following teams since 1927, the year it first became an exclusively NHL award, as shown in **Table 2**:

TABLE 2: STANLEY CUP FINALS

Season	Winner	Loser	Games
1926-27	Ottawa Senators	Boston Bruins	2-0
1927-28	New York Rangers	Montreal Maroons	3-2
1928-29	Boston Bruins	New York Rangers	2-0
1929-30	Montreal Canadiens	Boston Bruins	2-0
1930-31	Montreal Canadiens	Chicago Blackhawks	3-2
1931-32	Toronto Maple Leafs	New York Rangers	3-0
1932-33	New York Rangers	Toronto Maple Leafs	3-1
1933-34	Chicago Blackhawks	Detroit Red Wings	3-1
1934-35	Montreal Maroons	Toronto Maple Leafs	3-0
1935-36	Detroit Red Wings	Toronto Maple Leafs	3-1
1936-37	Detroit Red Wings	New York Rangers	3-2
1937-38	Chicago Blackhawks	Toronto Maple Leafs	3-1
1938-39	Boston Bruins	Toronto Maple Leafs	4-1
1939-40	New York Rangers	Toronto Maple Leafs	4-2
1940-41	Boston Bruins	Detroit Red Wings	4-0
1941-42	Toronto Maple Leafs	Detroit Red Wings	4-3
1942-43	Detroit Red Wings	Boston Bruins	4-0
1943-44	Montreal Canadiens	Chicago Blackhawks	4-0
1944-45	Toronto Maple Leafs	Detroit Red Wings	4-3
1945-46	Montreal Canadiens	Boston Bruins	4-1
1946-47	Toronto Maple Leafs	Montreal Canadiens	4-2
1947-48	Toronto Maple Leafs	Detroit Red Wings	4-0
1948-49	Toronto Maple Leafs	Detroit Red Wings	4-0
1949-50	Detroit Red Wings	New York Rangers	4-3
1950-51	Toronto Maple Leafs	Montreal Canadiens	4-1
1951-52	Detroit Red Wings	Montreal Canadiens	4-0
1952-53	Montreal Canadiens	Boston Bruins	4-1
1953-54	Detroit Red Wings	Montreal Canadiens	4-3
1954-55	Detroit Red Wings	Montreal Canadiens	4-3
1955-56	Montreal Canadiens	Detroit Red Wings	4-1
1956-57	Montreal Canadiens	Boston Bruins	4-1
1957-58	Montreal Canadiens	Boston Bruins	4-2
1958-59	Montreal Canadiens	Toronto Maple Leafs	4-1
1959-60	Montreal Canadiens	Toronto Maple Leafs	4-0
1960-61	Chicago Blackhawks	Detroit Red Wings	4-2

Season	Winner	Loser	Games
1961-62	Toronto Maple Leafs	Chicago Blackhawks	4-2
1962-63	Toronto Maple Leafs	Detroit Red Wings	4-1
1963-64	Toronto Maple Leafs	Detroit Red Wings	4-3
1964-65	Montreal Canadiens	Chicago Blackhawks	4-3
1965-66	Montreal Canadiens	Detroit Red Wings	4-2
1966-67	Toronto Maple Leafs	Montreal Canadiens	4-2
1967-68	Montreal Canadiens	St. Louis Blues	4-0
1968-69	Montreal Canadiens	St. Louis Blues	4-0
1969-70	Boston Bruins	St. Louis Blues	4-0
1970-71	Montreal Canadiens	Chicago Blackhawks	4-3
1971-72	Boston Bruins	New York Rangers	4-2
1972-73	Montreal Canadiens	Chicago Blackhawks	4-2
1973-74	Philadelphia Flyers	Boston Bruins	4-2
1974-75	Philadelphia Flyers	Buffalo Sabres	4-2
1975-76	Montreal Canadiens	Philadelphia Flyers	4-0
1976-77	Montreal Canadiens	Boston Bruins	4-0
1977-78	Montreal Canadiens	Boston Bruins	4-2
1978-79	Montreal Canadiens	New York Rangers	4-1
1979-80	New York Islanders	Philadelphia Flyers	4-2
1980-81	New York Islanders	Minnesota North Stars	4-1
1981-82	New York Islanders	Vancouver Canucks	4-0
1982-83	New York Islanders	Edmonton Oilers	4-0
1983-84	Edmonton Oilers	New York Islanders	4-1
1984-85	Edmonton Oilers	Philadelphia Flyers	4-1
1985-86	Montreal Canadiens	Calgary Flames	4-1
1986-87	Edmonton Oilers	Philadelphia Flyers	4-3
1987-88	Edmonton Oilers	Boston Bruins	4-0
1988-89	Calgary Flames	Montreal Canadiens	4-2
1989-90	Edmonton Oilers	Boston Bruins	4-1
1990-91	Pittsburgh Penguins	Minnesota North Stars	4-2
1991-92	Pittsburgh Penguins	Chicago Blackhawks	4-0
1992-93	Montreal Canadiens	Los Angeles Kings	4-1
1993-94	New York Rangers	Vancouver Canucks	4-3
1994-95	New Jersey Devils	Detroit Red Wings	4-0
1995-96	Colorado Avalanche	Florida Panthers	4-0
1996-97	Detroit Red Wings	Philadelphia Flyers	4-0
1997-98	Detroit Red Wings	Washington Capitals	4-0

INDIVIDUAL STATISTICS

Various career and season statistics are kept for each individual *NHL* player to keep track of his performance. The explanations below will help you become familiar with these statistics to help you understand measures of success for hockey players. Some of these statistics are tabulated for the best hockey players in the chapter entitled **NHL INDIVIDUAL RECORDS**.

GOALS (G): The number of times a player shoots the *puck* across the *goal line* between the *goalposts*.

ASSISTS (A): The number of times a player passes to a teammate who either scores or passes to another teammate who scores. A player who scores a goal cannot also be credited with an assist on the same goal.

POINTS (Pts): The number of goals plus the number of assists for a player.

SHOTS ON GOAL (SOG): A scoring attempt that is successfully blocked or otherwise prevented by a *goalie*; also called a *save*.

POWER PLAY GOALS (PP): The number of goals scored by a player when his team is on the *power play*.

SHORTHANDED GOALS (SH): The number of goals scored by a player when his team is *shorthanded*.

PENALTY MINUTES (PIM): The total amount of penalty time assessed to a player.

PLUS/MINUS (+/-): This statistic indicates the overall success of a player's team while he is on the ice. It is calculated by giving a player a *plus* (+1) when he is on the ice when an even-strength or shorthanded goal is scored by his team, and a *minus* (-1) when he is on the ice for an even-strength or shorthanded goal scored by the opposing team. These pluses and minuses are all added together to get the plus/minus statistic.

GOALS-AGAINST (GA): This statistic is the total number of goals a *goalie* has allowed other teams to score while he was in the goal.

GOALS-AGAINST AVERAGE (Avg.): Calculated by dividing goals-against for a goalie, excluding *empty-net goals*, by the number of games he played. The number of games used for this statistic is calculated by dividing the number of minutes played by 60 (the length of a full game).

SHUTOUTS (SO): This statistic is the number of times a goalie has played a complete game without allowing any goals to be scored.

DECIPHERING HOCKEY STATISTICS IN THE NEWSPAPER

Each day during the hockey season, most major newspapers contain lots of information about *NHL* hockey teams and players. There are team *standings*, showing how each team is performing in terms of wins and losses, and there are summaries of each game played the previous day called *game summaries* or *box scores*.

This section discusses how the team standings and game summaries appear in the newspaper.

TEAM STANDINGS: The team standings list each of the teams by total points earned during the season. *Points* are earned as follows:

• A team receives 2 points for each game it wins
• A team receives 1 point for each game that ends in a tie
• Zero points are awarded for losses

The information contained in these standings is described on the following page, using an example of NHL standings.

L - The number of losses a team has so far in the season.

Pts - Points earned by a team during the season to date.

Div. - A team's win-loss-tie record when it plays other teams in its division. Teams play more frequently against teams within their division than outside. Therefore, this statistic usually measures how well a team plays against its biggest rivals.

W - The number of wins a team has so far in the season.

T - The number of ties a team has so far in the season.

Home/Away - A team's win-loss-tie record when it plays on its home ice or on the road.

Eastern Conference Atlantic Division	W	L	T	Pts	GF	GA	Home	Away	Div.
New Jersey	48	23	11	107	225	166	29-10-2	19-13-9	13-8-3
Pittsburgh	40	24	18	98	228	188	21-10-10	19-14-8	11-8-5
Philadelphia	42	29	11	95	242	193	24-11-6	18-18-5	11-10-3
N.Y. Islanders	30	41	11	71	212	225	17-21-4	13-20-7	8-12-4
N.Y. Rangers	25	39	18	68	197	231	14-18-9	11-21-9	7-12-5

Northeast Division	W	L	T	Pts	GF	GA	Home	Away	Div.
Boston	39	30	13	91	221	194	19-16-6	20-14-7	12-7-5
Buffalo	36	29	17	89	211	187	20-13-8	16-16-9	11-7-6
Montreal	37	32	13	87	235	208	15-17-9	22-15-4	10-11-3
Ottawa	34	33	15	83	193	200	18-16-7	16-17-8	9-10-5
Toronto	28	40	14	70	180	212	16-22-3	12-18-11	7-14-3

Southeast Division	W	L	T	Pts	GF	GA	Home	Away	Div.
Washington	40	30	12	92	220	201	23-12-6	17-18-6	14-7-3
Carolina	33	41	8	74	200	219	16-18-7	17-23-1	11-10-3
Atlanta	31	40	11	73	196	223	18-16-7	13-24-4	10-12-2
Florida	24	43	15	63	203	256	11-24-6	13-19-9	9-10-5
Tampa Bay	17	55	10	44	151	269	11-23-7	6-32-3	7-12-5

GF - Goals For, or total goals scored by a team. An indicator of a team's offensive strength.

GA - Goals Against, or total goals scored against a team. An indicator of a team's defensive strength.

Western Conference Central Division	W	L	T	Pts	GF	GA	Home	Away	Div.
Detroit	44	23	15	103	250	196	25-8-8	19-15-7	15-5-4
St. Louis	45	29	8	98	256	204	26-10-5	19-19-3	13-8-3
Chicago	30	39	13	73	192	199	14-19-8	16-20-5	9-11-4
Columbus	30	43	9	69	194	237	16-20-5	14-23-4	9-13-2
Nashville	27	44	11	65	179	215	15-21-5	12-23-6	6-15-3

Northwest Division	W	L	T	Pts	GF	GA	Home	Away	Div.
Colorado	39	26	17	95	231	205	21-10-10	18-16-7	14-6-4
Minnesota	36	32	14	86	205	198	22-12-7	14-20-7	12-9-3
Edmonton	35	37	10	80	215	224	20-16-5	15-21-5	10-12-2
Calgary	26	41	15	67	217	252	18-17-6	8-24-9	7-12-5
Vancouver	25	43	14	64	224	273	15-22-4	10-21-10	8-12-4

Pacific Division	W	L	T	Pts	GF	GA	Home	Away	Div.
Dallas	49	22	11	109	242	167	26-8-7	23-14-4	14-7-3
Los Angeles	38	33	11	87	227	225	22-16-3	16-17-8	12-9-3
Phoenix	35	35	12	82	224	227	19-16-6	16-19-6	10-10-4
San Jose	34	38	10	78	210	216	17-19-5	17-19-5	8-12-4
Anaheim	26	43	13	65	205	261	12-23-6	14-20-7	6-12-6

GAME SUMMARIES: Being able to read a game summary or box score allows a reader to re-create the action and sequence of events that took place during a hockey game. There are several pieces of information contained in a box score, as explained below:

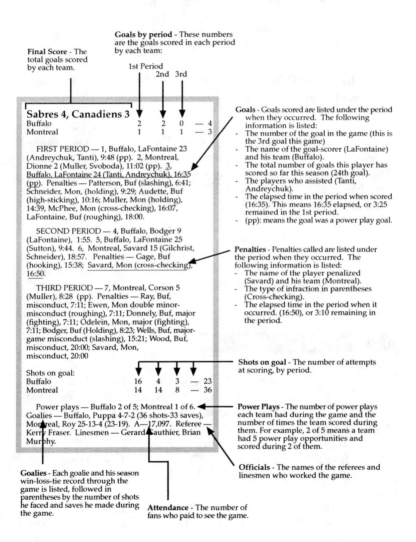

Goals by period - These numbers are the goals scored in each period by each team:

Final Score - The total goals scored by each team.

1st Period
2nd 3rd

Sabres 4, Canadiens 3

Buffalo	2	2	0	—	4
Montreal	1	1	1	—	3

FIRST PERIOD — 1, Buffalo, LaFontaine 23 (Andreychuk, Tanti), 9:48 (pp). 2, Montreal, Dionne 2 (Muller, Svoboda), 11:02 (pp). 3, Buffalo, LaFontaine 24 (Tanti, Andreychuk), 16:35 (pp). Penalties — Patterson, Buf (slashing), 6:41; Schneider, Mon, (holding), 9:29; Audette, Buf (high-sticking), 10:16; Muller, Mon (holding), 14:39, McPhee, Mon (cross-checking), 16:07, LaFontaine, Buf (roughing), 18:00.

SECOND PERIOD — 4, Buffalo, Bodger 9 (LaFontaine), 1:55. 5, Buffalo, LaFontaine 25 (Sutton), 9:44. 6, Montreal, Savard 15 (Gilchrist, Schneider), 18:57. Penalties — Gage, Buf (hooking), 15:38; Savard, Mon (cross-checking), 16:50.

THIRD PERIOD — 7, Montreal, Corson 5 (Muller), 8:28 (pp). Penalties — Ray, Buf, misconduct, 7:11; Ewen, Mon double minor-misconduct (roughing), 7:11; Donnely, Buf, major (fighting), 7:11; Odelein, Mon, major (fighting), 7:11; Bodger, Buf (Holding), 8:23; Wells, Buf, major-game misconduct (slashing), 15:21; Wood, Buf, misconduct, 20:00; Savard, Mon, misconduct, 20:00

Shots on goal:

Buffalo	16	4	3	—	23
Montreal	14	14	8	—	36

Power plays — Buffalo 2 of 5; Montreal 1 of 6. Goalies — Buffalo, Puppa 4-7-2 (36 shots-33 saves), Montreal, Roy 25-13-4 (23-19). A—17,097. Referee — Kerry Fraser. Linesmen — Gerard Sauthier, Brian Murphy.

Goals - Goals scored are listed under the period when they occurred. The following information is listed:
- The number of the goal in the game (this is the 3rd goal this game)
- The name of the goal-scorer (LaFontaine) and his team (Buffalo).
- The total number of goals this player has scored so far this season (24th goal).
- The players who assisted (Tanti, Andreychuk).
- The elapsed time in the period when scored (16:35). This means 16:35 elapsed, or 3:25 remained in the 1st period.
- (pp): means the goal was a power play goal.

Penalties - Penalties called are listed under the period when they occurred. The following information is listed:
- The name of the player penalized (Savard) and his team (Montreal).
- The type of infraction in parentheses (Cross-checking).
- The elapsed time in the period when it occurred. (16:50), or 3:10 remaining in the period.

Shots on goal - The number of attempts at scoring, by period.

Power Plays - The number of power plays each team had during the game and the number of times the team scored during them. For example, 2 of 5 means a team had 5 power play opportunities and scored during 2 of them.

Officials - The names of the referees and linesmen who worked the game.

Goalies - Each goalie and his season win-loss-tie record through the game is listed, followed in parentheses by the number of shots he faced and saves he made during the game.

Attendance - The number of fans who paid to see the game.

NHL INDIVIDUAL RECORDS

The following abbreviations will be used in this section:

A = assists	L = losses
Avg = average	Pts = points
Dec = decisions	SO = shutouts
G = goals	T = ties
GA = goals-against	Yrs = years
GP = games played	* = active player

CAREER LEADERS (as of the end of the 1997-98 season)

All-Time Career Goal-Scoring Leaders:

Player	Team	Yrs	GP	G
Wayne Gretzky*	Edmonton, LA, StL, NYR	19	1417	885
Gordie Howe	Detroit, Hartford	26	1767	801
Marcel Dionne	Detroit, LA, NY Rangers	18	1348	731
Phil Esposito	Chicago, Bos, NY Rangers	18	1282	717
Michael Gartner*	Wash, Min, NYR, Tor, Phx	19	1432	708
Mario Lemieux	Pittsburgh	12	745	613
Bobby Hull	Chi, Winnepeg, Hartford	16	1063	610
Dino Ciccarelli*	Min, Wash, Det, TB, Fla	18	1218	602
Jari Kurri	Edm, LA, NYR, Ana, Col	17	1251	601
Mark Messier*	Edmonton, NYR, Van	19	1354	597
Mike Bossy	NY Islanders	10	752	573

All-Time Career Assist Leaders:

Player	Team	Yrs	GP	A
Wayne Gretzky*	Edmonton, LA, StL, NYR	19	1417	1910
Paul Coffey*	Edm, Pitt, LA, Det, Hfd, Phi	18	1268	1090
Gordie Howe	Detroit, Hartford	26	1767	1049
Marcel Dionne	Detroit, LA, NY Rangers	18	1348	1040
Ray Bourque*	Boston	19	1372	1036
Mark Messier*	Edmonton, NYR, Van	19	1354	1015
Ron Francis*	Hartford, Pittsburgh	17	1247	1006
Stan Mikita	Chicago	22	1394	926
Bryan Trottier	NY Islanders, Pittsburgh	18	1279	901
Dale Hawerchuk	Wpg, Buf, StL, Phi	16	1188	891
Mario Lemieux	Pittsburgh	12	745	881

All-Time Career Point Leaders:

Player	Team	Yrs	GP	G	A	Pts
Wayne Gretzky*	Edm, LA, StL, NYR	19	1417	885	1910	2795
Gordie Howe	Det, Hfd	26	1767	801	1049	1850
Marcel Dionne	Det, LA, NYR	18	1348	731	1040	1771
Mark Messier*	Edmonton NYR, Van	19	1354	597	1015	1612
Phil Esposito	Chi, Bos, NYR	18	1282	717	873	1590
Mario Lemieux	Pittsburgh	12	745	613	881	1494
Paul Coffey*	Edm, Pitt, LA, Det, Hfd, Phi	18	1268	383	1090	1473
Stan Mikita	Chicago	22	1394	541	926	1467
Ron Francis*	Hfd, Pitt	17	1247	428	1006	1434
Bryan Trottier	NYIsl, Pitt	18	1279	524	901	1425
Ray Bourque*	Boston	19	1372	375	1036	1411
Steve Yzerman*	Detroit	15	1098	563	846	1409
Dale Hawerchuk	Win, Buf, StL, Phi	16	1188	518	891	1409

SINGLE-SEASON RECORDS (as of the end of the 1997-98 season)

Individual Regular-Season Goal Leaders:

Player	Team	Season	G
Wayne Gretzky*	Edmonton	'81-'82	92
Wayne Gretzky*	Edmonton	'83-'84	87
Brett Hull*	St. Louis	'90-'91	86
Mario Lemieux	Pittsburgh	'88-'89	85
Phil Esposito	Boston	'70-'71	76
Alexander Mogilny*	Buffalo	'92-'93	76
Teemu Selanne*	Winnepeg	'92-'93	76
Wayne Gretzky*	Edmonton	'84-'85	73
Brett Hull*	St. Louis	'89-'90	72
Wayne Gretzky*	Edmonton	'82-'83	71
Jari Kurri	Edmonton	'84-'85	71
Mario Lemieux	Pittsburgh	'87-'88	70
Bernie Nicholls*	Los Angeles	'88-'89	70
Brett Hull*	St. Louis	'91-'92	70

Individual Regular-Season Assist Leaders:

Player	Team	Season	A
Wayne Gretzky*	Edmonton	'85-'86	163
Wayne Gretzky*	Edmonton	'84-'85	135
Wayne Gretzky*	Edmonton	'82-'83	125
Wayne Gretzky*	Los Angeles	'90-'91	122
Wayne Gretzky*	Edmonton	'86-'87	121
Wayne Gretzky*	Edmonton	'81-'82	120
Wayne Gretzky*	Edmonton	'83-'84	118
Wayne Gretzky*	Los Angeles	'88-'89	114
Mario Lemieux	Pittsburgh	'88-'89	114
Wayne Gretzky*	Edmonton	'87-'88	109
Wayne Gretzky*	Edmonton	'80-'81	109
Wayne Gretzky*	Los Angeles	'89-'90	102
Bobby Orr	Boston	'70-'71	102

Individual Regular-Season Point Leaders:

Player	Team	Season	G	A	Pts
W. Gretzky*	Edmonton	'85-'86	52	163	215
W. Gretzky*	Edmonton	'81-'82	92	120	212
W. Gretzky*	Edmonton	'84-'85	73	135	208
W. Gretzky*	Edmonton	'83-'84	87	118	205
M. Lemieux	Pittsburgh	'88-'89	85	114	199
W. Gretzky*	Edmonton	'82-'83	71	125	196
W. Gretzky*	Edmonton	'86-'87	62	121	183
M. Lemieux	Pittsburgh	'87-'88	70	98	168
W. Gretzky*	Los Angeles	'88-'89	54	114	168
W. Gretzky*	Edmonton	'80-'81	55	109	164
W. Gretzky*	Los Angeles	'90-'91	41	122	163
M. Lemieux	Pittsburgh	'95-'96	69	92	161

PLAYOFF RECORDS (as of the end of the 1997-98 season)

All-Time Playoff Goal Leaders:

Player	Team	Yrs	GP	G
Wayne Gretzky*	Edmonton, LA, StL	16	208	122
Mark Messier*	Edmonton, NY Rangers	17	236	109
Jari Kurri	Edm, LA, NYR, Ana, Col	15	200	106
Glenn Anderson	Edmonton, Tor, NYR, StL	15	225	93
Mike Bossy	NY Islanders	10	129	85
Maurice Richard	Montreal	15	133	82
Jean Beliveau	Montreal	17	162	79
Dino Ciccarelli*	Minn, Wash, Detroit	14	141	73
Claude Lemieux*	Montreal, NJ, Colorado	13	179	73
Esa Tikkanen*	Edm, NYR, StL, Van, Wash	13	186	72
Bryan Trottier	NY Islanders, Pittsburgh	17	221	71
Mario Lemieux	Pittsburgh	7	89	70
Brett Hull*	Calgary, St. Louis	13	108	69

All-Time Playoff Assist Leaders:

Player	Team	Yrs	GP	A
Wayne Gretzky*	Edmonton, LA, StL	16	208	260
Mark Messier*	Edmonton, NY Rangers	17	236	186
Paul Coffey*	Edm, Pitt, LA, Det, Phi	15	189	136
Jari Kurri	Edm, LA, NYR, Ana, Col	15	200	127
Glenn Anderson	Edmonton, Tor, NYR, StL	15	225	121
Doug Gilmour*	StL, Calgary, Tor, NJ	14	152	117
Ray Bourque*	Boston	18	168	116
Larry Robinson	Montreal, Los Angeles	20	227	116
Bryan Trottier	NY Islanders, Pittsburgh	17	221	113
Denis Savard	Chicago, Montreal	16	169	109
Larry Murphy*	LA, Wash, Min, Pit, Tor, Det	17	190	109
Denis Potvin	NY Islanders	14	185	108
Adam Oates*	Det, StL, Bos, Wash	11	126	100

All-Time Playoff Point Leaders:

Player	Team	Yrs	GP	G	A	Pts
W. Gretzky*	Edm, LA, StL	16	208	122	260	382
Mark Messier*	Edm, NYR	17	236	109	186	295
Jari Kurri	Edm, LA, NYR, Ana, Col	15	200	106	127	233
Glenn Anderson	Edm, Tor, NYR, StL	15	225	93	121	214
Paul Coffey*	Edm, Pitt, LA, Detroit, Philly	15	189	59	136	195
Bryan Trottier	NYI, Pitt	17	221	71	113	184
Jean Beliveau	Montreal	17	162	79	97	176
Denis Savard	Chi, Montreal	16	169	66	109	175
Doug Gilmour*	StL, Cgy, Tor, NJ	14	152	54	117	171
Denis Potvin	NY Islanders	14	185	56	108	164
Mike Bossy	NY Islanders	10	129	85	75	160
Gordie Howe	Det, Hartford	20	157	68	92	160
Bobby Smith	Mtl, Minn	13	184	64	96	160

GOALTENDING STATISTICS (as of the end of the 1997-98 season)

All-Time Shutout Leaders:

Player	Team	Yrs	GP	SO
Terry Sawchuck	Det, Bos, Tor, LA, NYR	21	971	103
G. Hainsworth	Montreal, Toronto	11	464	94
Glenn Hall	Detroit, Chicago, St. Louis	18	906	84
Jacques Plante	Mtl, NYR, StL, Tor, Bos	18	837	82
Tiny Thompson	Boston, Detroit	12	553	81
Alex Connell	Ott, Det, NYA, Maroons	12	417	81
Tony Esposito	Montreal, Chicago	16	886	76
Lorne Chabot	NYR, Tor, Mtl, Chicago, MM, NY Americans	11	411	73
Harry Lumley	Det, NYR, Chi, Tor, Bos	16	804	71
Roy Worters	Pitt, NY Americans, Mtl	12	484	66
Turk Broda	Toronto	14	629	62

Single Season Regular-Season Shutout Leaders:

Player	Team	Season	GP	SO
G. Hainsworth	Montreal	1928-29	44	22
Alex Connell	Ottawa	1925-26	36	15
Alex Connell	Ottawa	1927-28	44	15
Hal Winkler	Boston	1927-28	44	15
Tony Esposito	Chicago	1969-70	76	15
G. Hainsworth	Montreal	1926-27	44	14
Clint Benedict	Mtl. Maroons	1926-27	44	13
Alex Connell	Ottawa	1926-27	44	13
G. Hainsworth	Montreal	1927-28	44	13
John Roach	NY Rangers	1928-29	44	13
Roy Worters	NY Americans	1928-29	44	13
Harry Lumley	Toronto	1953-54	70	13
Dominik Hasek*	Buffalo	1997-98	72	13

All-Time Win Leaders:

Player	Wins	GP	Dec	L	T	%
Terry Sawchuck	447	971	950	330	173	.562
Jacques Plante	434	837	827	246	147	.614
Tony Esposito	423	886	881	306	152	.567
Glenn Hall	407	906	897	327	163	.545
Grant Fuhr*	382	806	757	271	104	.573
Patrick Roy*	380	717	691	224	87	.613
Andy Moog*	372	713	669	209	88	.622
Rogie Vachon	355	795	773	291	127	.541
Gump Worsley	334	861	831	349	148	.491
Harry Lumley	333	804	802	326	143	.504
Mike Vernon*	331	624	605	201	73	.607

Single-Season Goals-Against Average Leaders since 1935:

Player	Team	Season	GP	GA	SO	Avg
Dave Kerr	NYR	1939-40	48	77	8	1.54
Frankie Brimsek	Boston	1938-39	43	68	10	1.56
Tiny Thompson	Boston	1935-36	48	82	10	1.68
Al Rollins	Toronto	1950-51	40	70	5	1.77
Tony Esposito	Chicago	1971-72	48	82	9	1.77
Lorne Chabot	Chicago	1934-35	48	88	8	1.80
Tiny Thompson	Boston	1937-38	48	89	7	1.80
Harry Lumley	Toronto	1953-54	69	128	13	1.86
Jacques Plante	Montreal	1955-56	64	119	7	1.86
Jacques Plante	Toronto	1970-71	40	73	4	1.88
Martin Brodeur*	New Jersey	1996-97	67	120	10	1.88
Ed Belfour*	Dallas	1997-98	61	112	9	1.88

THE NHL DRAFT

The *NHL Draft* is held once a year in June, about 7-10 days after the last game of the *Stanley Cup Finals*. Amateur hockey players from all over the world who are at least 18 years old can be selected by each of the NHL teams. The order of selection is in reverse order of the teams' end-of-season records (ignoring the results of any *post-season* play). If any teams are tied, the tiebreakers include comparing their respective number of wins or the results of head-to-head play between the tied teams. Recently, the NHL proposed a lottery system among the non-*playoff* teams to determine this order of selection. This prevents a team from purposely losing games to end up with the worst record and the top pick.

There are currently 9 *rounds* in the draft; this means each team has the opportunity to select 9 players, one per round. There is a player that will be drafted *1st overall*; this means he was the first choice in the first round made by the NHL team that drafted first (or had the worst end-of-season record). This player is usually the best player of all those available that year, and he is expected to help the worst team improve in the next season and ultimately enhance the competition in the NHL. You might also hear a player referred to as "the Philadelphia Flyers' 1st pick in 1985"; this signifies the player was the first player chosen by that team, even if his team did not choose first within that round.

Whenever an *expansion team* is added to the league, a separate *expansion draft* is held. Existing teams are permitted to "protect" a certain limited number of their key players, but must leave most members of their team exposed. The expansion teams can then select from among the unprotected players to create their teams. This helps new teams to start their first season with some experienced and talented NHL players which allows for better competition against the older, established teams in the league. It still usually takes a few years for an expansion team to improve its season record. However, after a few years of doing poorly, an expansion team will have had several opportunities to draft high in the June draft, selecting from among the best young players each year. Such a team is likely to improve quickly.

NHL ALL-STAR GAME
& TEAMS

ALL-STAR GAME

The *National Hockey League*'s annual *All-Star Game* is held in late-January, midway through the *regular season*. The game is generally played on a Saturday, and the location changes each year. Since 1985, the *starting lineups* on each of the two teams (*Eastern Conference* versus *Western Conference*, formerly known as the *Wales Conference* versus *Campbell Conference*) have been selected by a vote of the fans. The rest of the players on each team are selected by the NHL's Hockey Operations Department which consults with senior general managers. Currently this committee must ensure that each NHL team has at least one representative, but as the number of teams in the NHL continues to grow through expansion, this is getting more difficult to do.

The first official All-Star Game was hosted by the Toronto Maple Leafs in 1947. Until 1968 (except for two seasons), the *Stanley Cup* defending champion hosted the All-Star Game, playing against the selected team of All-Stars. For the first 19 years, the game was played before the start of the regular season, shifting to mid-season in 1967. In 1979 and 1987, the NHL All-Star team broke from its usual interconference format and played opposite a team from the Soviet Union. No game was held in 1995 due to a work stoppage, and in 1998, the All-Star battle was held between players from North America and those from the rest of the world.

The first unofficial All-Star game was also played in Toronto in February 1934, following an unfortunate incident. In 1933, *Eddie Shore*, the most feared defenseman in hockey, became frustrated by his opponents' incredible stickhandling which denied his Boston Bruins the puck during a *power play* opportunity. On one play, after he was mercilessly thrown to the ground, he rose up and skated full force into an innocent *Ace Bailey*, flipping him over his shoulder. Bailey hovered between life and death with a serious head injury. He recovered, but never played hockey again. The game in 1934 was intended as a benefit for Bailey; Shore was booed on center ice until Bailey embraced him in forgiveness.

ALL-STAR TEAMS
To clarify a point of frequent confusion, it is different for a player to play in the All-Star Game than it is for a player to be selected to the All-Star Team. The players who participate in the All-Star Game are chosen a month before the mid-season point by the fans and a committee of general managers strictly to play in the All-Star Game. The players who are selected to the All-Star Team are chosen at the end of each season by the Professional Hockey Writers' Association; they do not play a game. For the All-Star Team, 12 players are selected, 2 representatives for each of the 6 player positions (First-Team All-Stars and Second-Team All-Stars). They are each chosen because they have excelled in their particular position during the season.

THE HOCKEY HALL OF FAME

The *Hockey Hall of Fame* was founded in 1943 in Toronto, Ontario, Canada. Its original location was in the city's Exhibition Park. Built at a cost of $500,000, it officially opened on August 26, 1961. A new center opened on June 18, 1993 on the corner of Young and Front Streets in downtown Toronto. Those honored are selected annually by hockey experts and generally inducted each September. It generally takes 3 years after retirement for a player or referee to be eligible for membership, but this period can be shortened in exceptional cases as determined by the Hockey Hall of Fame Board of Directors. Inductees are in one of three categories: players, *referees* and builders. The builders group includes professional and amateur league and club executives, team owners and other nonplayers who have distinguished themselves through their help in the development and promotion of the sport.

The *United States Hockey Hall of Fame*, located in Eveleth, Minnesota, opened in June 1973 to honor notable American players and pay tribute to hockey's innovators. A committee selects new members each year from among players, coaches, referees and administrators to be inducted in October.

NHL HOCKEY TROPHIES
(excluding NHL sponsor-affiliated awards)

HART MEMORIAL TROPHY: Awarded to the *NHL's* Most Valuable Player as selected by a vote of the *Professional Hockey Writers' Association* at the end of the *regular season*. The original Hart Trophy was donated in 1923 by Dr. David A. Hart, father of Cecil Hart, former manager-coach of the *Montreal Canadiens*. The award was presented to the NHL in 1960 after the original Hart Trophy was retired to the *Hockey Hall of Fame*. *Wayne Gretzky* has won this award with the Edmonton Oilers and Los Angeles Kings 9 times.

ART ROSS TROPHY: Awarded to the player who leads the NHL in *points* scored during the regular season. Ties for the lead are decided by giving the trophy first to the player with the most *goals*, then to the one with the fewer number of games played, then to the player who scored his first goal of the season at the earlier date. The trophy was presented to the NHL in 1947 by Art Ross, the former manager-coach of the Boston Bruins. Won by Wayne Gretzky 10 times, *Gordie Howe* of Detroit and *Mario Lemieux* of Pittsburgh each 6 times, *Phil Esposito* of Boston 5 times, and *Stan Mikita* of Chicago 4 times.

MAURICE "ROCKET" RICHARD AWARD: Awarded to the NHL's top goal-scorer during the regular season. New for the 1998-99 season, this award is dedicated to *"Rocket" Richard*, the first player ever to score 50 goals in a season.

JAMES NORRIS MEMORIAL TROPHY: Awarded to the league's best *defenseman*. Selected by a vote of the Professional Hockey Writers' Association at the end of the regular season. Presented in 1953 in honor of the late owner-president of the Detroit Red Wings by his four children. Won by *Bobby Orr* of Boston 8 times, *Doug Harvey* of Montreal 7 times and *Ray Bourque* of Boston 5 times.

VEZINA TROPHY: Awarded to the *goalie* voted most valuable by the general managers of each NHL team. Until the 1981-82 season, the trophy was awarded to the goalie for the team which had the fewest goals scored against it during the regular season. The trophy was presented to the NHL in 1926-27 by the owners of the Montreal Canadiens in memory of *Georges Vezina*, an outstanding former Canadien goalkeeper. Won by *Jacques Plante* of Montreal and St. Louis 7 times, Bill Durnan of Montreal 6 times and *Terry Sawchuck* of Detroit and Toronto and *Dominik Hasek* of Buffalo each 4 times.

CALDER MEMORIAL TROPHY: Awarded to the league's outstanding *rookie*, "the player selected as the most proficient in his first year of competition" in the NHL. Selected by a vote of the Professional Hockey Writers' Association at the end of the regular season. Originated in 1937 by *Frank Calder*, the first NHL *President*. After his death in 1943, the NHL presented the Calder Memorial Trophy in his memory. Players who are older than 26 prior to the start of the season or that participated in more than 25 games in any preceding season or in six or more games in each of any two preceding seasons are not eligible. Top rookies were named but no trophy was presented from 1932-1937.

CONN SMYTHE TROPHY: Awarded to the *Most Valuable Player* in the *Stanley Cup Playoffs*. Selected by a vote of the Professional Hockey Writers' Association at the end of the *Stanley Cup Finals*. The trophy was presented by Maple Leaf Gardens, Ltd. in 1964 to honor the Toronto Maple Leafs' former coach, manager, president and owner-governor. The first 29 trophies awarded went to Canadian players. The first time an American was honored was in 1994 when Brian Leetch of the New York Rangers won it.

LADY BYNG TROPHY: Awarded to the player combining the highest type of sportsmanship and gentlemanly conduct plus a high standard of playing ability. Selected by a vote of the Professional Hockey Writers' Association at the end of the regular season. Lady Byng, wife of the then Governor-General of Canada, presented the trophy to the NHL in 1925. *Frank Boucher* of the New York Rangers was given the original award to keep after winning it 7 times in 8 seasons. Lady Byng donated another trophy in 1936.

BILL MASTERTON TROPHY: Awarded by the Professional Hockey Writers' Association to "the NHL player who exemplifies the qualities of perseverance, sportsmanship and dedication to hockey." Presented in 1968 by the NHL Writers' Association in memory of the Minnesota North Star player who died that year from an injury sustained in a hockey game.

KING CLANCY MEMORIAL TROPHY: Awarded "to the player who best exemplifies leadership qualities on and off the ice and has made a noteworthy humanitarian contribution in his community." It was presented by the NHL's Board of Governors in 1988 in memory of *Frank "King" Clancy* of the Toronto Maple Leafs, honoring his service as a player, coach, *referee* and executive.

WILLIAM M. JENNINGS AWARD: Awarded to the goalie(s) on the team which gives up the fewest goals during the regular season. A goalie must play at least 25 games to be eligible. The trophy was presented to the NHL in 1982 by the NHL's Board of Governors in memory of William M. Jennings, who was instrumental in the league's *expansion* from six teams to 21. Multiple recipients from the same team are possible each year.

FRANK J. SELKE AWARD: Awarded to the *forward* "who best excels in the defensive aspects of the game." Selected by a vote of the Professional Hockey Writers' Association at the end of the regular season. The trophy was presented to the NHL in 1977 by the NHL's Board of Governors in honor of Frank J. Selke, who spent more than 60 years in the game as coach, manager and front-office executive.

LESTER B. PEARSON AWARD: Awarded to the NHL's outstanding player of the year as selected by a vote of the *NHL's Players' Association (NHLPA)*. It was presented by the NHLPA in 1970-71 in honor of the late Prime Minister of Canada. Won by Wayne Gretzky of Edmonton 5 times, Mario Lemieux of Pittsburgh 4 times and *Guy Lafleur* of Montreal 3 times.

PLUS/MINUS AWARD: This annual award goes to the player who, after playing a minimum of 60 games, leads the NHL in the *plus/minus* statistic at the end of the regular season. A plus/minus award has been presented since 1982-83.

JACK ADAMS AWARD: Awarded since 1974 by the NHL Broadcasters' Association to the "NHL coach adjudged to have contributed the most to his team's success." It is presented in the memory of the longtime coach and general manager of the Detroit Red Wings.

LESTER PATRICK TROPHY: Awarded for outstanding service to hockey in the U.S. Eligible recipients are players, *officials*, coaches, executives and referees. Selected by a rotating 8-member committee of individuals involved with hockey. Presented by the New York Rangers in 1966 to honor the memory of its long-time general manager and coach. There can be multiple winners each year.

PRESIDENT'S TROPHY: Presented annually by the President of the NHL to the club finishing the regular season with the best overall record. It was presented by the NHL Board of Governors to the NHL in 1985-86.

PRINCE OF WALES TROPHY: Since 1981-82, the trophy has gone to the winner of the *Wales Conference* (which was renamed the *Eastern Conference* starting with the 1993-94 season) who advances to the Stanley Cup Finals. The Prince of Wales donated the trophy to the NHL in 1924. From 1927-1938, it was presented to the team finishing first in the American Division of the NHL. From 1938-1967, it was given to the first-place team in the one-division league. From 1967-1981 it was awarded to the first-place finisher in the East Division and from 1981-93 to the playoff champion in the Wales Conference. Since 1993-94 it has gone to the Eastern Conference champion.

CLARENCE S. CAMPBELL BOWL: Named for the former president of the NHL, this award originally was given to the champions of the West Division. Since 1981-82, it has gone to the team advancing to the Stanley Cup Finals as the winner of the *Campbell Conference*, which was renamed the *Western Conference* starting with the 1993-94 season.

HOCKEY PERSONALITIES: PAST AND PRESENT

In this section you will find short biographies on some of the most famous hockey players of the past as well as current stars; also included are the *Presidents* and *Commissioner* of the *NHL*. Although there have been many great hockey players over the years, limited space prevents us from listing them all. Please do not be disappointed if some of your favorites are not listed. All statistics in this section are current through the end of the 1997-98 *regular season*. The following key of abbreviations applies to the entries that follow:

A = active player
All-Star Team = combines First Team and Second Team selections for each player
Art Ross Trophy = scoring champion
Calder Trophy = Rookie of the Year
Conn Smythe = Playoff MVP
D = defenseman
F = forward
G = goalie
HF = inducted into Hall of Fame
Lady Byng Trophy = for sportsmanship
MVP = Most Valuable Player
Norris Trophy = best defenseman
R = retired
Top 50 = The Hockey News Top 50 NHL players of all-time (1997)
Vezina Trophy = best goalie
WHA = World Hockey Association

BELIVEAU, JEAN: (F, HF, Top 50) When he refused to give up his amateur status (and the $20,000 salary that it brought him), the *Montreal Canadiens* purchased the entire Quebec Senior League and turned it from an amateur into a professional league. This left him no choice but to join Montreal in 1953, where he went on to become the then-highest scoring center in NHL history with 1219 points and 507 goals in 18 seasons. During his career he went to the playoffs 17 times (16 consecutive) and played on 10 Stanley Cup championship teams. Beliveau was selected playoff MVP in 1965; he was also selected to the *All-Star Team* 10 times and won the *Hart Trophy* as the NHL's MVP twice.

BETTMAN, GARY: (Commissioner, A) He was selected as the first Commissioner of the NHL in February 1993, replacing interim President Gil Stein. As the Senior Vice-President and General Counsel of the National Basketball Association he successfully marketed the sport of basketball internationally. In his first year, Bettman made good his promise to bring the league into the mainstream of American sports by landing the NHL's first network television deal (a 5-year $155 million contract with Fox Network) and several major sponsors (including Anheuser-Busch Cos. and Nike, Inc.). Although Bettman did not know much about hockey when he started, tough negotiating skills served him well in labor disputes with on-ice *officials* and players early in his tenure.

BOSSY, MIKE: (F, HF, Top 50) He started a 10-year career that was shortened by back problems by winning the *Calder Trophy* in 1977-78 and setting a record for most goals by a *rookie* (67) which was not broken until 1992-93 by *Teemu Selanne*. In his first 6 seasons he totaled 365 *goals* and 693 *points* (an average of 61 goals and 116 points a season), on his way to accumulating a career 573 goals. He set NHL records for *right wings* in 1981-82 when he scored 64 goals and 83 *assists* for 147 points which stood until *Jaromir Jagr* broke it in 1995-96. Bossy would have won the scoring trophy that year but for *Wayne Gretzky's* record-breaking 212 points and 92 goals. The next year, he was awarded his first of 3 *Lady Byng Trophies*.

Bossy was an instrumental force in the New York Islanders' 4 consecutive Stanley Cup championships (scoring the series winning goal in both 1982 and 1983!), winning the *Conn Smythe* award in 1982 (their 3rd championship) and scoring 17 *playoff* goals the next year. In fact, his career playoff goal total of 85 is 5th best of all-time. He scored over 50 goals in 9 consecutive seasons, a record which remains today, and over 60 in 5 seasons out of 10, a record now shared with Gretzky; in 1983, he became the first player to score 60 goals 3 years in a row. Bossy was selected to the *All-Star Team* 8 times.

BOURQUE, RAY: (D, A) In the first of his 19 consecutive years with the Boston Bruins (1979-80), Bourque was named *Rookie of the Year* (*Calder Trophy*). A perennial *All-Star* who was even named All-Star *MVP* in 1996, he has won the *Norris Trophy* for best *defenseman* an impressive 5 times (1986-87, 1987-88, 1989-90,

1990-91 and 1993-94). Bourque, who has served as either captain or co-captain of the Bruins since 1985, holds the franchise's all-time record for most *points* (1,411) and most *assists* (1,036 – which is also 5th best all-time). Bourque has speed and agility, and ranks behind only *Paul Coffey* with the most goals, assists and points for defensemen.

BOWMAN, SCOTTY: (Coach, HF) The most successful *coach* in *NHL* history, Bowman has won more games than any other coach (1,057) and more *playoff* games (194) than any coach in the history of major team sports. Bowman certainly got an early start, coaching a junior team of 20-year-olds when he was just 21. In his 26-year career, 3 different NHL teams he coached have won 8 *Stanley Cups* in 12 finals appearances. With Bowman at the helm, the *Montreal Canadiens* won 5 Cups including 4 straight from 1976-79, and the Pittsburgh Penguins won in 1991 and 1992. To add to his incredible career, he coached the Detroit Red Wings to 2 straight Stanley Cups in 1997 and 1998, their first in 42 years. These teams all had one thing in common: Bowman the master motivator in charge, driving his players hard and emphasizing teamwork. He is also known as one of the first coaches to exploit individual *matchups* on the ice.

BURE, PAVEL: (F, A) Dubbed the "Russian Rocket" because of his blazing speed on the ice, Bure is one of the most explosive scorers in professional hockey. As a teenage rising star in the Soviet Union, he helped the national team win a world hockey title before defecting to North America in 1991, signing a contract with the NHL's Vancouver Canucks. He quickly established himself in his first season, scoring 34 goals in only 65 games on his way to winning the *Calder Trophy*. In each of his first 2 full seasons Bure scored 60 goals, enough to lead the league in 1993-94 and become a First-Team *All-Star*. His end-to-end *rushes* during the 1994 NHL *playoffs* introduced him to a growing television audience and netted him 16 goals to lead all playoff scorers that year. Bure led the NHL in goals scored in 1997-98 with 51, and he was the leading scorer in the 1998 Olympics with 9 goals, leading Russia to the silver medal. His contract pays him the average of the top 3 *forwards* in the league.

COFFEY, PAUL: (D, A, Top 50) This goal-scoring *defenseman* and perennial *All-Star* set and broke several records since joining the NHL in 1980. To this day he retains the defensemen records for longest scoring streak (28 games in 1985-86), most *goals* in a single season (48 in 1985-86), most career goals (383), most career *assists* (1090) and most career *points* (1473). He led all NHL defensemen in scoring numerous seasons, and consistently ranked in the top 6 among all players from 1983-86 and in 1988-89. Coffey won the *Norris Trophy* three times (1984-85, 1985-86 and 1994-95). He is currently ranked 2nd all-time in assists, an incredible feat for a defenseman. The Edmonton Oiler team he played on won 3 *Stanley Cups* (1983-84, 1985-86 and 1986-87), before he was traded to the Pittsburgh Penguins in 1987, where he won his 4th Stanley Cup championship in 1990-91. Midway through the 1991-92 season, he was again traded, this time to the Los Angeles Kings where he was reunited with his former Edmonton teammate *Wayne Gretzky*. Since then, Coffey has played for several other teams.

DIONNE, MARCEL: (F, HF, Top 50) This *center* is the third all-time leading scorer and *goal*-scorer after *Wayne Gretzky* and *Gordie Howe* with 1771 *points* and 731 goals. In 1984-85, he became the first player to score 100 points in 8 seasons. In 1986-87, he became only the second player in history after Howe to attain 1600 career points; in 1987-88 he joined Howe and *Phil Esposito* in passing the 700 career goal mark, and he joined Gretzky and Howe in passing the 1000 assist mark. He won the *Art Ross Trophy* in 1979-80, the *Lady Byng Trophy* twice (1975 and 1977) and he was selected to the *All-Star Team* 4 times. He started his career with the Detroit Red Wings from 1971 to 1975, then played with the Los Angeles Kings until he was traded to the New York Rangers during the 1986-87 season. He retired at the end of the 1988-89 season after 19 outstanding seasons.

DRYDEN, KEN: (G, HF, Top 50) This *goalie*, often referred to as a human octopus, was the backbone of 6 *Stanley Cup* championships for the *Montreal Canadiens* in the 1970s, including 4 consecutive titles. He won both the *Calder Trophy* and the *Conn Smythe Trophy* as *playoff MVP* in his *rookie* season (1970-71). He was named to the *All-Star Team* 6 times, and won or shared the *Vezina Trophy* for best goalie 5 times. He led the league in *shutouts* 4 times, ending his short 7-year, 397-game career with 46 shutouts and a low 2.24 *goals-against average*; his average for 112 *playoff* games was 2.40 goals-against. Dryden surprised everyone by retiring at the height of his career at the age of 31, moving to England with his family to write a book on his hockey experience before returning to live in Toronto in 1982.

ESPOSITO, PHIL: (F, HF, Top 50) "Espo" retired in January 1981 after 18 seasons as the then-second highest scorer in NHL history after *Gordie Howe* with 1590 *points* (717 *goals* and 873 *assists*). He was the first player to score over 100 points in a season and he surpassed 55 goals a season 5 consecutive times. Surprisingly Espo did not show an interest in playing hockey until he was a teenager. His NHL career began with the Chicago Blackhawks, but in 1967 he was traded to the Boston Bruins where he spent 8 $^1/_2$ seasons. He sparked the Bruins to two *Stanley Cups* championships after a 29-year wait in 1970 and 1972. His greatest season came in 1970-71 when he established a record season-high of 152 points including a record 76 goals. Both these records would stand a full decade until they were broken by *Wayne Gretzky*. Esposito won the *Art Ross Trophy* 5 times and the *Hart Trophy* twice. In 1975 he was traded to the New York Rangers, where he rarely played up to his old Boston form. He retired in 1981, ending a career that included being selected to the *All-Star Team* 8 times. After a few brief stints as coach and general manager of the New York Rangers in the late 1980s, in 1992 he became part-owner and the first general manager of the Tampa Bay Lightning *expansion team*. His brother, Tony was one of the NHL's greatest *goalies*.

ESPOSITO, TONY: (G, HF) He made a brief appearance in the NHL in 1968 with the *Montreal Canadiens* before being signed by the Chicago Blackhawks in 1969. In his first full season, he won the *Calder Trophy*, the *Vezina Trophy* for best *goalie* with his 2.17 *goals-against average*, was named to the *All-Star Team* and established a modern-day NHL record with 15 *shutouts* which still stands today. He shared the Vezina Trophy 2 more times, was an All-Star 4 more times and helped Chicago win 9 *division* titles (including 4 consecutive). When he retired in 1984 he had 76 career shutouts, a modern-day *goalie* record.

FEDEROV, SERGEI: (F, A) After playing for 4 years on the Russian national team with the likes of now-NHL stars *Pavel Bure* and Alexander Mogilny, Federov defected to the United States during the 1990 Goodwill Games (at age 21) and was drafted by the Detroit Red Wings. This versatile player improves every year and enjoyed a particularly stellar season in 1993-94 when he won 3 major awards – the *Hart Trophy* as league *MVP* (the first Russian ever to win it), the *Selke Trophy* for best defensive *forward* (which he won again in 1996) and the *Pearson Award*. That year

Federov, with his speed and creativity, garnered 120 *points*, the 2nd best total in the league behind *Wayne Gretzky*. In 1996-97, Federov was an integral part of Detroit's first *Stanley Cup* in 42 years and in 1997-98, when Detroit won the first back-to-back championships since the Penguins (1991, 1992), he received an immediate $12 million bonus for getting them to the *Eastern Conference* finals. Combined with his $14 million signing bonus and $2 million salary, he was one of the richest players in the league that year; his $28 million windfall was more than the L.A. Kings' entire $24 million payroll! That year he also played for the Russian team that brought home a silver medal from the Olympics. Federov's personal life came into the spotlight in 1997 when the then-27 year old's relationship with 16-year old tennis star Anna Kournikova came under scrutiny, and he was criticized by other Russian players for not accompanying them on a tour of their homeland with the Stanley Cup.

FORSBERG, PETER: (F, A) This Swedish League Player of the Year (1993-94) was selected 6th overall by the Philadelphia Flyers. He was traded to the Quebec Nordiques (now the Colorado Avalanche) along with 5 other players, 2 *draft* picks, cash <u>and</u> future consideration for *Eric Lindros*, though some scouts believe his game is better than Lindros'. A smooth skater with explosive speed, there is little Forsberg can't accomplish on the ice. He controls the puck well, is an outstanding playmaker who relishes contact and he has the ability to think a play or two ahead of others on the ice (the same trait that made *Wayne Gretzky* so successful). In his *rookie* year Forsberg won the *Calder Memorial Trophy* (1994-95), then was named an *All-Star* twice and was a member of the 1996 *Stanley Cup* championship team. He was instrumental in the Avalanche becoming the 1st team to win 4 straight *division* titles since the Edmonton Oilers of the mid-1980s and he was also part of the Swedish team that took home the gold medal in the 1994 Olympics. Forsberg is the first hockey player to appear on a Swedish postage stamp.

GARTNER, MIKE: (F, A) Despite the fact that Gartner's 19-year NHL career has taken him from the Washington Capitals to the Minnesota North Stars to the New York Rangers to the Toronto Maple Leafs to the *expansion* Phoenix Coyotes (and he may soon be traded again!), his ability to score consistently remained unaffected. Gartner is a finesse player, known for his remarkable speed, flawless technical form and durability (this 38-year old

89

did not miss a single game over the last 2 seasons). He holds the NHL career record for most consecutive 30-*goal* seasons (15 from 1979-80 to 1993-94) and the most 30+ goal seasons (17), and is 5th all-time in goals scored (708). This 7-time *All-Star* was also named All-Star *MVP* in 1993 and shares an All-Star Game record for most goals scored (4 in 1991). Gartner is a born-again Christian.

GRETZKY, WAYNE: (F, A, Top 50) He is known as "The Great One" and he has the statistics to back up the name. His pro career began in the *WHA* with the Indianapolis Racers; his first pro contract was signed in 1978-79 when he was only 17 for $1.7 million. After only 8 games he was sold to the Edmonton Oilers, signing a 21-year contract for $5 million. In 1982, at the age of 21, he renegotiated his contract, receiving over $1 million a year

Wayne Gretzky.

and becoming the then-highest-paid player in NHL history. Gretzky was well worth it.

In his *rookie* year, he led the league in scoring and *assists*, won the *Hart Trophy* as NHL MVP and the *Lady Byng Trophy*. In his second NHL season he established records for most *points* (164) and most *assists* (109) becoming the first player to average 2 points a game. In his third season, 1981-82, he rewrote the records books: he scored 50 *goals* in his first 39 games, becoming the first to break *Rocket Richard's* record (50 games); then he eclipsed *Phil Esposito's* single-season goal-scoring record of 76 goals (78 games) when by February 1982 he had scored 79 goals in just 64 games; he then finished the season with an astounding 92 goals, 120 assists and 212 points, all of which were single-season records. He later broke his own single-season record for points, setting the current standard at 215; the NHL single-season goals record still stands at 92, and the only player to break the single-season assists record has been Gretzky himself, 5 different times. In 1988, he was traded to the Los Angeles Kings, where he spent 9 years setting and breaking more records and taking them to the finals in 1993. He was then signed by the New York Rangers as a *free agent* in 1996 after part of a year with the St. Louis Blues.

Toward the end of the 1993-94 season, Gretzky reached one of the only milestones left — he broke *Gordie Howe's* record for career goals when he scored his 802nd on March 23, 1994. It took him only 15 years compared to Howe's 26 years. He had already bypassed Howe's 1850 career points total in 1989 to become the all-time leader on his way to becoming the first player to reach 2000 points. His current total of 2795 is untouchable; the next active player on the all-time list, *Mark Messier*, has 1612. He also bypassed Howe's record of 1049 career assists and currently has 1910. He has had nine 50+ goal seasons; and in 4 of these he scored over 70. It is not surprising Gretzky's name appears beside nearly every NHL record that relates to scoring or which involves a *center*, for both the *regular season* and playoffs. During his 19 seasons he has won the *Hart Trophy* 9 times (8 consecutive), the *Art Ross Trophy* 10 times (7 consecutive), was the captain of 4 *Stanley Cup* championship teams, was awarded the *Conn Smythe Trophy* twice (1985, 1988), the *Lady Byng* 4 times, was selected to the *All-Star Team* 14 times and played in 16 All Star Games. Gretzky is married to actress Janet Jones, and his brother Brent was a center for the Tampa Bay Lightning.

HALL, GLENN: (G, HF, Top 50) This *goalie* started his NHL career with the Detroit Red Wings by winning the *Calder Trophy* in 1955-56. He went on to win the *Vezina Trophy* 3 times and to be selected to the *All-Star Team* in 11 of his 14 seasons in the NHL. Hall led the NHL in *shutouts* for 6 seasons and still holds the record for the most consecutive complete games by a goaltender (502), ending his career in 1971 with an excellent 2.51 *goals-against-average*. He was traded to Chicago in his third season and spent 10 years there. In 1961, he helped the Blackhawks win their first *Stanley Cup* in 23 years by holding a *Montreal Canadiens* team that included *Jean Beliveau, Rocket Richard* and "Boom Boom" Geoffrion scoreless for 135 minutes and 26 seconds. In 1968, he led his third team, the expansion St. Louis Blues into the first of 3 consecutive Stanley Cup Finals where despite their loss in 4 straight games, he still emerged as the *playoff MVP* winning the *Conn Smythe Trophy*. Until the second half of his final season, Hall played without a mask, yet did not miss one minute of play in 7 years (1955-1962), a time when NHL teams carried only one goalie. He went on to become the Calgary Flames' goaltending consultant for the last 13 years.

HARVEY, DOUG: (D, HF, Top 50) This all-around athlete (baseball and football) was a 7-time winner of the *James Norris Trophy* as the NHL's leading *defenseman* and named to the *All-Star Team* 11 times in his 17 seasons with the NHL that began in 1947. He played the *point* on the *Montreal Canadiens'* awesome *power play* during the 1950s that could score numerous *goals* against *shorthanded* teams; this was the team that caused the NHL to change its rules and permit a player penalized by a *minor penalty* to return to the ice as soon as a single goal is scored against his team. With the Canadiens he won 6 *Stanley Cups* (5 consecutive). In 1961 he was traded to the New York Rangers and, after a stint in the minors, finished his NHL career with the St. Louis Blues in 1969 by helping them reach the Stanley Cup Finals. Harvey died in 1989 at the age of 65.

HASEK, DOMINIC: (G, A) Hasek's unorthodox style (he flops like a fish, flails, sprawls, abandons his stick and relies on his terrific leg reflexes to stop the puck!) has not stopped "the Dominator" from being considered among the world's best *goalies* (an opinion espoused by none other than *Wayne Gretzky*). He is consistently at the top of the NHL in *save percentage*, leading the league for 5 consecutive seasons since 1993-94 while winning the *Vezina Trophy* 4 times in 5 years. Hasek also won the *Hart Memorial Trophy* the same years as his 3rd and 4th Vezinas (quite an accomplishment for any player, let alone a goalie) just after signing a 3-year $23-million contract with the Buffalo Sabres in 1996-97. His 4-year extension is worth $32 million more. In 1998, Hasek added an Olympic gold medal to his list of accomplishments, playing an instrumental role that included 20 *saves* in the victory game for his native Czechoslovakia; he was honored by Czech astronomers who named an asteroid after him. That same year, despite setting an NHL-record 6 *shutouts* in a month, he failed to tie *Tony Esposito's* modern-day single season record of 15 by just 2 *shutouts*, a feat he is sure to try again. Hasek, the son of a uranium miner, began playing goal as a toddler; his first pair of skates was a pair of shoes with blades screwed into the soles. He does not appreciate it when his teammates tease him about resembling Kramer on Seinfeld. They may be treading more lightly since 1997 when Hasek was suspended for 3 *playoff* games and fined $10,000 by the NHL for grabbing a reporter who had written a critical column. His notorious temper notwithstanding, he is gentle with children and the founder of a hockey program for needy youngsters.

HOWE, GORDIE: (F, HF, Top 50) He is considered the most enduring player in the history of professional hockey having played 32 seasons (26 with the NHL, 6 with the *World Hockey Association (WHA)*) before retiring (for the second and final time) in 1980 at the age of 52. At the time he retired, he held the all-time NHL records for *goals, assists* and *points*; he is still in second place in goals and points behind only *Wayne Gretzky*. He held the all-time record for goals scored for 31 years until 1994 when Gretzky surpassed Howe's career total of 801. Howe established many NHL records, some of which he still retains including most assists (1049) by a *right wing*. Combining his NHL and WHA statistics, including *playoff* games, Howe played in 2421 games where he collected 1071 goals, 1518 assists, 2589 points and 2419 *penalty minutes*. In his 25 years with the Detroit Red Wings he was named to the *All-Star Team* a record 21 times.

After sitting out 2 years, he returned in 1973 to play with his sons Marty and Mark in the WHA for 6 more seasons; he then finished with one more year in the NHL with the Hartford Whalers. During a 1950 Stanley Cup game, Howe collided with an opponent and crashed head-on into the sideboards, suffering

Gordie Howe.

a severe brain injury. Although he hung between life and death,
the injury left him only with a slight facial tic, which is why his
teammates called him "Blinky." He won the *Art Ross Trophy* 6
times (including 4 consecutive seasons) and was a 6-time winner
of the *Hart Trophy* as *MVP*. On October 3, 1997, Howe played a
shift for Detroit's *IHL* minor league team making him the first
individual to appear in a professional hockey game for each of 6
consecutive decades (1940s-1990s)

HULL, BOBBY: (F, HF, Top 50) He entered the NHL in 1957 with
the Chicago Blackhawks, and during his first 15 years, he helped
a *franchise* that was losing money become one of the richest in
the NHL. In 1972 he accepted $1 million to play for the
Winnepeg Jets of the *World Hockey Association* (*WHA*) where he
played 7 $^1/_2$ seasons. He was traded to the Hartford Whalers late

in the 1979-80 season and even played a few games with *Gordie Howe* before retiring in 1980 at the age of 41. In his 23-year career he amassed 1018 *goals* and 2071 *points*, including his WHA statistics. He was, in fact, the most dominant scorer of the 1960s and 70s, cracking the 50-goal barrier 5 times with Chicago and 4 more times with the Jets. In 1974-75 he scored a record 77 goals in 78 games. He retains the

Bobby Hull.

NHL record for the most career goals by a *left wing* (610) to this day, a total which places him 7th on the current all-time list.

He did not, however, become a prolific scorer until his third season, when he improved on the *slap shot*, a technique developed by "Boom Boom" Geoffrion of the *Montreal Canadiens* and Andy Bathgate of the New York Rangers, and which became Hull's calling card. Hull also added a curve to the blade of his stick which increased the speed of the puck. The slap shot, which he shot at 118.3 miles per hour (or 35 mph above the league average), and the fact that he was the fastest skater in hockey (28.3 mph with the puck, 29.7 mph without it) coupled with his blonde, good looks earned him the nickname Golden Jet. He led the NHL in goals scored 7 different seasons, won the *Art Ross Trophy* 3 times, the *Hart Trophy* twice, the *Lady Byng Trophy* once and was selected to the *All-Star Team* 12 times.

HULL, BRETT: (F, A) This *right wing* is following in his father's skate strides, although he hardly knew *Bobby Hull* until he was grown (the result of a bitter divorce where Brett went to live with his mother). He developed from a lazy, pudgy kid into one of the most prolific and charismatic hockey players all on his own. Hull is one of the NHL's most feared snipers, appearing from out of nowhere to score. In his first 13 seasons in the NHL, he amassed 553 *goals* (13th in league history and 7th among active players) and is also one of only 3 players (with *Wayne Gretzky* and *Mario Lemieux*) to ever score 80+ goals in a single season (86 in 1991-92). He won the *Lady Byng Trophy* (1990) and the *Hart Trophy* (1991), and has been an All-Star 3 times to date. The Dallas Stars ended his 10-year stay with the St. Louis Blues when they signed him to a 3-year $17.5 million contract in 1998. Hull is known for his brutal honesty, and though he once claimed

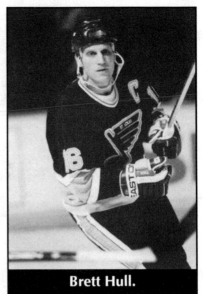

Brett Hull.

he would never marry nor have children, he and his wife are the proud parents of 3 kids.

JAGR, JAROMIR: (F, A) Overshadowed by superstar teammate *Mario Lemeiux* for many years, Jagr developed into an offensive force to be reckoned with. Born in Czechoslovakia, he was chosen in the 1st round of the 1990 *draft* (5th overall pick) by the Pittsburgh Penguins and quickly played a role in the team's back-to-back *Stanley Cup* victories. A powerful skater who is almost impossible to catch, his wrist shot is one of the *NHL*'s best. Jagr's skills landed him 2 *Art Ross Trophies* (1995 and 1998) as the league's top scorer, the first European-trained player ever to win the award. A member of the Czech team that won the gold medal at the 1998 Olympics, Jagr is most easily recognized by his long black hair flowing from under his helmet.

KARIYA, PAUL: (F, A) One of the most fluid *skaters* and skilled *passers* in the *NHL*, Kariya became the 2nd highest-paid hockey player ever in 1998 when he signed a 2-year $14 million contract with the Anaheim Mighty Ducks after a bitter 32-game holdout. His abilities have always created great expectations. At age 19, he helped Canada win the silver medal at the 1994 Olympics and was *drafted* that year in the 1st round (4th overall pick) by the Mighty Ducks. Kariya soon became the youngest *captain* in the

NHL and scored 50 *goals* in his first full season. He finished runner-up for the *Hart Trophy* in 1996-97 when he lead the NHL in game-winning goals, and won the *Lady Byng Trophy* two years in a row (1996, 1997). A *cross-check* to the jaw gave Kariya a severe concussion in 1998, prematurely ending his season.

KURRI, JARI: (F, R, Top 50) In his first 10 seasons, starting in 1980-81, he was instrumental in helping *Wayne Gretzky* lead the Edmonton Oilers to 4 *Stanley Cup* championships; Kurri and the Oilers won a 5th title without the Great One in 1989-90. He was reunited with Gretzky on the Los Angeles Kings in 1992, helping also to lead that team into the Stanley Cup Finals only to lose to the *Montreal Canadiens* in 1993. Since then he was signed as a *free agent* with the Anaheim Mighty Ducks (1996) and finished his career with the Colorado Avalanche (1997). This *goal*-scorer broke the 50-goal barrier 4 consecutive years, which included a 71-goal season in 1984-85, becoming only the third player in history to pass the 70-goal mark after Gretzky and *Phil Esposito*. He is third all-time in *playoff* goals (106), 4th on the all-time playoff *assists* list (127) and third behind Gretzky and *Mark Messier* with 233 all-time playoff *points*. Although he has not won an *Art Ross Trophy*, he has come in second in points to Gretzky on two occasions, has won one *Lady Byng Trophy* and has made 8 *All-Star Game* appearances. He retired in 1998 as the highest-scoring European player in NHL history. Kurri brought home a bronze medal from the 1998 Olympics for his native Finland, where he plans to "live like a retired person." However, a Finnish charity that raises money for a children's hospital lured him back to play hockey for at least 4 more years.

LAFLEUR, GUY: (F, HF, Top 50) This *right wing*'s *goal* scoring led the *Montreal Canadiens* to 4 consecutive *Stanley Cup* championships (1976-1979). He played on the 1976-77 Canadien team that boasts the best single-season record in NHL history, 60-8-12. Lafleur dominated the late 1970s, setting the record for 6 consecutive 50+ goal seasons (which was later broken by *Mike Bossy* in 1983-84) on his way to 3 consecutive *Art Ross Trophies* in 1976, 1977 and 1978. During those years he also picked up 2 *Hart Trophies* (1977 and 1978) and won the *Conn Smythe Trophy* (1977). He was selected to the *All-Star Team* 6 times before he stopped playing in 1984. After a 3 ½-year pause and his induction into the *Hall of Fame*, he joined the New York Rangers in 1988 and was traded to the Quebec Nordiques the next season. He was the youngest to score 400 career goals and achieve 1000 *points* in the NHL, retiring in 1991 as one of the best right wings of all time.

LECLAIR, JOHN: (F, A) At 6'3", 226 lbs., this Philadelphia Flyer is nearly impossible to move away from the *net* where he scrounges for *rebounds* and *deflections* that lead to *goals*. His tactics seem to be working, as he scored 50+ goals 3 straight years (1995-98). His ability to score on the *power play* led him to an NHL-leading +44 *plus/minus* rating in 1996-97. LeClair was originally drafted by the *Montreal Canadiens* in 1987 where he played in relative obscurity before being traded to the Flyers in 1995. Today he is the *left wing* on the "Legion of Doom" line along with *center Eric Lindros*. One of the top U.S.-born players in the NHL (he's from Vermont), LeClair was an integral part of the U.S. team that won the first-ever World Cup in 1996-97. The John LeClair Foundation he started in 1993 hosts golf tournaments which have raised over $500,000 for Vermont children's charities.

LEMIEUX, MARIO: (F, HF, Top 50) Nothing short of spectacular when he was healthy, Lemieux was unfortunately besieged by health problems throughout his career ranging from anemia to severe back problems to Hodgkin's disease (a form of cancer). He started his NHL career by scoring a *goal* on his first shot of his first game. The number one overall *draft pick* in 1984-85 did not disappoint becoming only the 3rd *rookie* in NHL history to reach 100 *points* and earning the *Calder Trophy*. He went on to win the *Art Ross Trophy* and the *Hart Trophy* in 1987-88, breaking *Wayne Gretzky's* string of 7 consecutive Art Ross and 8 consecutive Hart Trophies. Lemieux would win the Hart Trophy twice more (1993, 1996) and the Art Ross 5 more times (1989, 1992, 1993, 1996, 1997). He led the Pittsburgh Penguins to their first *Stanley Cup* in 1991, and after an incredible comeback from back surgery (missing 16 games), led them to a 2nd title in 1992. In both years he was awarded the *Conn Smythe Trophy* for his efforts, becoming only the 2nd player to win it in consecutive seasons. Even after missing 24 games while undergoing radiation treatment in 1992-93, he sparked his team to an NHL-record 17-game winning streak when he returned to the lineup and won his 4th *scoring title* in 6 years. In 1994-95, this superstar decided to sit out the season to recover from lingering fatigue.

Mario Lemieux.

He returned with a vengeance in 1995-96, scoring 69 goals and 161 points during the *regular season*, followed by 27 points in 18 *playoff* games in reaching the *Eastern Conference* finals. He was honored with both the Art Ross and Hart Trophies that year. His next and final season, Lemieux once again led the league with 122 points taking home his 6th Art Ross. All in all, he led the league in goals 3 times (85 in 1988-89, 70 in 1987-88 and 69 in 1995-96) and in points 6 times. When he retired he had accumulated 613 goals, 881 assists, and 1494 points in only 745 *regular-season* games, making him the only player to average over 2 points per game in his career (2.01). He was selected to the *All-Star Team* 8 times in his 12 NHL seasons and twice named male athlete of the year by the Canadian press (1988, 1993). Lemieux is remembered not just for his leadership and skill as a player, but for the class with which he presented himself both on and off the ice.

LINDROS, ERIC: (F, A) The number-one overall *draft pick* chosen by the Quebec Nordiques in 1991 was this then-19 year old *center* who was expected to rival the likes of *Wayne Gretzky* and *Mario Lemieux*. When he refused to play for Quebec, a battle for his services was waged between the New York Rangers and the Philadelphia Flyers. An arbitrator's decision approved a trade to the Flyers for 6 players (including *All-Star Peter Forsberg*), 2 first-round draft choices and a pile of cash. Although plagued by injuries throughout his career, the 6' 4", 235-pound Lindros has been spectacular when healthy. Injuries to his knees (he wears braces on both), groin pulls and major bruises have eaten into several of his seasons. However, when he was able to play 73 games in the 1995-96 season, he scored 115 *points* and won the *Hart Trophy* as league *MVP* and the *Lester B. Pearson Award*. Named the Flyers' youngest *captain* ever in 1994 at age 21, Lindros has been criticized as a weak leader for the team's perennial poor performance in the *playoffs*. This did not prevent him from getting a one-year contract extension in 1998 for $8.5 million.

MESSIER, MARK: (F, A, Top 50) Having led the New York Rangers in 1994 to its first *Stanley Cup* championship in 54 years (and his 6th), Messier can truly be acknowledged as one of the winningest players of all-time. He was an integral member of the powerhouse Edmonton Oiler team of the 1980s that won 4 Stanley Cups with *Wayne Gretzky* and *Jari Kurri*, winning a *Conn Smythe Trophy* in 1983-84. A year after Gretzky left to play for the Los Angeles Kings, Messier led the Oilers to their fifth title in 1989-90, earning himself the *Hart Trophy* in the process. Traded to the Rangers in 1991-92, he immediately won his second Hart Trophy on his way to his sixth 100+ *point* season. During the 1994 *playoffs* with the Rangers facing elimination in a game against their cross-town rival New Jersey Devils, in a feat of legendary proportions, Messier brashly guaranteed a victory, and won the game by scoring a *hat trick*! In 1997, the Rangers let this *free agent* go and the Vancouver Canucks signed him to a 3-year $20 million deal. Called "the greatest leader in professional sports today" by his former coach Mike Keenan, Messier has scored an incredible 295 career points in the *playoffs*, second all-time only to Gretzky. He is also 10th all time in *goals*, 6th all time in *assists* and a 12-time *All-Star Game* participant. His brother, 2 cousins and brother-in-law have all played in the NHL.

MIKITA, STAN: (F, HF, Top 50) This center for the Chicago Blackhawks played with *Bobby Hull* and was one of the leading scorers of his era along with Andy Bathgate and *Gordie Howe*. He won the *Art Ross Trophy* 4 times, the *Hart Trophy* twice, the *Lady Byng Trophy* twice and was selected to the *All-Star Team* 8 times. In 1967, he became the first player in NHL history to win all three awards in a single year, a feat he repeated the next year. In a 22-season career that ended in 1980, he amassed 541 *goals* and 926 *assists* for 1467 *points* and helped bring Chicago to the *Stanley Cup* finals for the 5th time with a victory in 1960-61. In 1972 Mikita founded the American Impaired Hearing Association to help hard of hearing youngsters.

ORR, BOBBY: (D, HF, Top 50) Six knee operations cut his brilliant NHL career to 10 years with the Boston Bruins and a few games with the Chicago Blackhawks. When he retired at the age of 30, Orr held or shared 12 individual NHL records. He was the first player to score 100 *assists* (102) in a single season, an incredible feat considering he was a *defenseman*. To this day he retains the NHL's single-season records for most assists by a defenseman (102) and most *points* by a defenseman (139). He was named *Rookie of the Year*, winning the *Calder Trophy* in 1967. Orr scored a remarkable 915 points in 657 games; he was the only defenseman ever to win the *Art Ross* scoring championship and he did it twice. He also won the *Norris Trophy* as best defenseman 8 consecutive years through the 1974-75 season and is credited with revolutionizing the role of the

Bobby Orr.

defenseman with slick passing, end-to-end dashes and playmaking. It was his overtime goal that brought the 1970 Bruins their first Stanley Cup in 29 years; that goal was his 9th *playoff* goal and 20th point, both of which were then-playoff records. In 1970 he became the first player to win 4 trophies in one year: the Art Ross, the Norris, the *Hart* and the *Conn Smythe*. Orr went on to be the first NHL player to win the Hart Trophy 3 consecutive years. He was also named to 8 consecutive *All-Star Teams* and won the Conn Smythe Trophy again in 1972. He was the first player to be officially represented in contract negotiations by an agent, and today is himself one of the game's most powerful agents. His Boston-based agency, Woolf Associates, recruits players as young as 14.

PLANTE, JACQUES: (G, HF, Top 50) In the 10 years he spent with the *Montreal Canadiens*, they won 6 *Stanley Cup* championships (including 5 consecutive titles from 1956-1960). He won the *Vezina Trophy* for best *goalie* 7 times (including 5 in a row) and was selected as a member of the *All-Star Team* 7 times. Plante was only the 4th *goalie* to win the *Hart Trophy* (1962). Over his 21-year career he had an outstanding 2.38 *goals-against-average* in 837 games and recorded 82 *shutouts*. In 1959 he was the first goalie to popularize wearing a *face mask*, despite management's opposition, after an injury to his face required stitches. He was traded to the New York Rangers in 1963 and spent 1½ years there. The St. Louis Blues lured him out of retirement in 1968, to win his 7th Vezina Trophy and lead that team to two consecutive *division* titles at the age of 40. He then spent 3 seasons with the Toronto Maple Leafs from 1970-1973 and ended his career in the *World Hockey Association (WHA)* with the Edmonton Oilers in 1974-75. Plante died in 1986.

POTVIN, DENIS: (D, HF, Top 50) This goal-scoring *defenseman* was the captain of the New York Islanders team that won 4 consecutive *Stanley Cup* championships from 1980-1983. This highly-touted first pick of the 1973 *draft* started his 15-year career by winning the *Calder Trophy* (1973-74) and went on to win 3 *Norris Trophies* (1976, 1978 and 1979). Potvin broke several of *Bobby Orr*'s NHL records for defensemen in 1985-86 (915 career *points* and 271 career *goals*), then broke Brad Park's record for career *assists* (684) in 1986-87, then topped it off by becoming the first defenseman ever to score 300 goals. When he retired at the age of 34, he held the NHL's defensemen records for most goals

(310), most assists (742) and most points (1052).   He was also selected to the *All-Star Team* 7 times.

PRESIDENTS: The first *President* of the NHL was *Frank Calder;* appointed in 1917; he served until his death in 1943. *Red Dutton* took over as President through the war years of 1943-1946. He was succeeded by *Clarence Campbell,* who was President from 1946-1976. *John A. Ziegler, Jr.* became the 4th President in the NHL's 61-year history in 1977. He was a Michigan-born lawyer, who played amateur hockey. In October 1992, he stepped down, and *Gil Stein* acted as the interim president of the NHL until the NHL appointed its first *Commissioner, Gary Bettman,* in February of 1993.

RICHARD, MAURICE ("ROCKET"): (F, HF, Top 50) This famed *Montreal Canadiens'* ambidextrous *right wing's* 544 career *goals* (in 18 NHL seasons) stood as the record until broken by *Gordie Howe.* He was voted into the *Hall of Fame* only 9 months after his 1960 retirement. The Rocket was the 1st player in the NHL to score 50 goals during a season (1944-45) and he remains the only player to achieve that in a 50-game schedule. He was selected to the *All-Star Team* 14 times. In 1955, NHL *President Campbell* issued him a multiple-game suspension for punching a *linesman.* This came one week before the end of a season in which he was vying to win the scoring championship and included the *Stanley Cup playoffs,* precipitating the infamous Ste. Catherine Street riots in downtown Montreal which caused over $1 million of damage. In 1998, the 76-year old Richard waged a battle against a rare form of abdominal cancer, the same year the NHL dedicated an annual award given in his honor to the league's top goal scorer.

ROY, PATRICK: (G, A, Top 50) As a rookie in 1985-86, he became the youngest player ever to be selected as *playoff MVP,* winning the *Conn Smythe Trophy* and the *Stanley Cup* championship at the age of 20. To date, this impressive *goalie* has won the *Vezina Trophy* 3 times (1989, 1990 and 1992) and was selected to the *All-Star Team* 7 times. He boasted the NHL's best *goals-against-average* for 3 years (2.47 in 1988-89, 2.53 in 1989-90 and 2.36 in 1991-92). In 1992-93, he helped the *Montreal Canadiens* win its 24th Stanley Cup, winning the Conn Smythe Trophy again.

SAKIC, JOE: (F, A) Selected by the Quebec Nordiques as an underage junior in the 1st round of the 1987 *draft,* Sakic's career really began to flourish in the 1990s. Long considered one of the league's best playmakers, he has recently become one of the game's best shooters, known for his quick release and patience with the puck. He plays his best under the pressure of important games. An *All-Star* every year from 1990-98, Sakic was instrumental in the Colorado Avalanche's 1996 *Stanley Cup* victory as the leading scorer in the *playoffs*, winning the *Conn Smythe Trophy*. Sakic also has excelled in international play as a gold medallist in the 1994 World Hockey Championship and as a member of Team Canada for the 1996 World Cup. One of the most respected players in the NHL, this soft-spoken leader has been his team's *captain* from 1990 to the present.

SAWCHUCK, TERRY: (G, HF, Top 50) He played 21 NHL seasons for the Detroit Red Wings (1950-1955, 1957-1964, 1968), Boston Bruins (1955-1957), Toronto Maple Leafs (1964-1967), Los Angeles Kings (1967) and the New York Rangers (1969-to his death off the ice in 1970). He is considered one of the greatest *goalies* in history having played more seasons, more games and accumulated more *shutouts* (103) than any other goalie. He is the only goalie to ever reach the 100 shutout mark and this record stands to this day, as does his record for the most games appeared in by a goaltender (971). When he won the *Calder Trophy* in 1950-51, Sawchuck became the 1st player to win a *rookie* award in 3 different professional leagues (the USHL in 1948 and AHL in 1949). In each of his first 3 seasons his *goals-against-average* was less than 2.00. He went on to win 5 *Stanley Cup* championships, to win or share the *Vezina Trophy* 4 times and to be selected to the *All-Star Team* 7 times. To this day, he tops the list of all-time win leaders with 435.

SELANNE, TEEMU: (F,A) In his NHL debut in the 1992-93 season with the Winnepeg Jets, the "Finnish Flash" won the *Calder Trophy*, set new NHL *rookie* records for most *goals* (76) and most *points* (132), and was selected to the *All-Star Team*. His single-season 76-goal total is still the 6th highest in NHL history. Despite a sophomore slump in 1993-94 (scoring only 25 goals in an injury-plagued 51 games) Selanne's play was good enough to earn another All-Star Team selection and 4 *All-Star Game* appearances from 1993 to 1997. In 1996 he was traded to the Anaheim Mighty Ducks where his career continues to flourish. He was tied for the league lead in goals in 1997-98 (52), which was also a Mighty Duck franchise record. Selanne's brilliant play and unbelievable speed on the ice translated into international success where he was instrumental in the silver medal victory of his native Finland in the 1998 Olympics. Selanne, who was a kindergarten teacher in Finland for 3 years, enjoys music, fishing and jogging, is interested in magic and card tricks and collects antique cars (he has 25!). With a two-year contract extension through 2001-02 worth $19.5 million, Selanne is likely to add a few more cars to his collection.

SHORE, EDDIE: (D, HF, Top 50) This explosive player is generally regarded as the greatest and most feared *defenseman* of all time. He played 13 1/2 seasons for the Boston Bruins starting in 1929, and is credited with lifting that *franchise* from last place to 2nd place in their *division* and developing a loyal following for the team. He played his last 1/2 season with the New York Americans. Before retiring, he won the *Hart Trophy* 4 times (the only defenseman to do so) 2 *Stanley Cup* championships and was voted to the *All-Star Team* 8 times. In 1933, he was responsible for fracturing *Ace Bailey*'s skull and ending Bailey's hockey career. Shore died in 1985.

VEZINA, GEORGES: (G, HF) He played with the *Montreal Canadiens* for 15 years from 1910-1925 in an era when *goalies* could not sprawl on the ice to *block* shots (the rule wasn't changed until 1922). He helped his team win 2 NHA (National Hockey Association) championships, 3 NHL championships and 2 *Stanley Cups*. He played in his last game in November 1925, and died of tuberculosis four months later at the age of 39. The *Vezina Trophy* honoring the most outstanding goalies in the NHL is awarded annually in his memory.

YZERMAN, STEVE: (F, A) Capping a 15-year career of individual accomplishments, Yzerman led the Detroit Red Wings to their 2nd straight *Stanley Cup* in 1998 after a 42-year drought. His 24 *points* in the 1998 *playoffs* led the NHL and won him the *Conn Smythe Award*. Yzerman is the longest-serving team *captain* in NHL history, leading the team for the last 12 years. *Drafted* by the Red Wings in the 1st *round* in 1983 (4th overall *pick*) at the tender age of 18, this *center* went on to score 1,000 points in fewer games than any player other than *Wayne Gretzky*. He led his team in scoring 8 years in a row, including 6 straight 100+ *point* seasons and 155 points in 1988-89 when he won the *Lester B. Pearson Award*. Yzerman is known for being a sensational skater, effective *penalty killer*, and gritty leader willing to sacrifice his body for the team cause. **105**

GLOSSARY

Adams Division: with the *Patrick Division* made up the *Wales Conference* until the 1992-93 season; renamed the *Northeast Division* of the *Eastern Conference* starting with the 1993-94 season.

All-Star Game: a mid-season *exhibition game* pitting selected stars of the *Eastern Conference* against selected stars of the *Western Conference*.

assist: the pass or passes which immediately precede a successful scoring attempt; a maximum of two assists are credited for one *goal*.

attacking zone: the area between the opponents' *blue line* and their *goal*.

backcheck: an attempt by a player, on his way back to his *defensive zone*, to regain the *puck* from the opposition by *checking* or harassing an opponent who has the puck.

backhand shot: a shot or pass made with the stick from the left side by a right-handed player or from the right side by a left-handed player.

beat the defense: to get by one or both of the *defensemen*.

beat the goalie: to outwit the *goalie* and score a *goal*.

behind the net: the area of ice behind the *goal cage* is legal territory.

blind pass: to pass the *puck* without looking.

blue lines: two blue, 12-inch wide lines running parallel across the ice, each 60 feet from the *goal*; they divide the *rink* into three *zones* called the *attacking*, *defending* and *neutral* (or center) *zones*; *defending blue line* is the line closer to a player's own *net*; *attacking blue line* is the one farther from his net; used in determining *offsides*.

boarding or board-checking: a *minor penalty* which occurs when a player uses any method (*body checking*, *elbowing* or *tripping*) to throw an opponent violently into the boards; if an injury is caused, it becomes a *major penalty*.

boards or board wall: a wooden wall 3 ½ to 4 feet high which surrounds the *rink* to keep the *puck* and players from accidentally leaving the rink and injuring spectators; all rinks have shatterproof glass that rises above the boards to provide additional protection.

body check: when a hockey player bumps or slams into an opponent with either his hip or shoulder (the only legal moves) to block his progress or throw him off-balance; it is only allowed against an opponent in control of the *puck* or against the last player to control it.

break: a chance to start a *rush* when the opposing *forwards* are caught out of position.

breakaway or breakout: a fast break in which an attacker with the *puck* skates in alone on the *goalie*, having gotten past or clear of the *defensemen*, trapping the opponents behind the play.

breaking pass: a pass to a teammate who is trying for a *breakaway*.

butt-ending: a *minor penalty* which occurs when an opponent is hit with the top of a player's hockey stick.

Campbell Conference: one of the two conferences in the *NHL* that contained the *Norris* and *Smythe Divisions* until 1992-93; the other conference was the *Wales Conference*; these were renamed the *Eastern* and *Western Conferences* in 1993.

carom: a rebound of the *puck* off the *boards* or any other object.

center or center forward: the center player in the *forward line* who usually leads his team's attack when they are trying to score a *goal*; he takes part in most of the *face-offs*; he controls the *puck* and tries to score or pass it to a teammate who is in a better position to score a goal.

center face-off circle: a circle, measuring 30 feet in diameter, at the center of the ice where the *puck* is dropped in a *face-off* to start the game and to restart the game after a *goal* has been scored.

center ice: the area between the two *blue lines*, also called the *neutral zone*.

centering pass: a pass from an attacking player towards the middle of the ice to a teammate with a better angle at the *goal*.

center line: a red, 12-inch wide line across the ice midway between the two *goals*.

charging: a *minor penalty* which occurs when a player makes a deliberate move of more than two steps when *body checking* an opponent; if serious injury is caused or blood is drawn it becomes a *major penalty*.

check or checking: any defensive or guarding tactic used by hockey players accomplished by moving their bodies against an opponent to get the *puck* away; there are two main types of *checks*: *stick check* and *body check*; these are only allowed against a player in control of the puck or against the last player to control it; checking with too many steps or strides becomes *charging*.

clearing the puck: getting the *puck* out of one's own *defensive zone*.

clearing the zone: when a defending player sends the *puck* out of the *attacking zone*, all the attacking players must leave or *clear* the zone to avoid being called *offsides* when the puck reenters the zone.

cover: when a player stays close to an opponent to prevent him from receiving a pass or making a play on offense.

crease lines: the red lines that form the semi-circular area with a 6-foot radius in front of the *goal* called the *goal crease*.

cross bar: the horizontal bar that connects the top of the two *goalposts*.

cross-checking: a *minor penalty* which occurs when a player holds his stick in both hands and drives the shaft into an opponent; a *stick check* where a player has both hands on the stick and no part of the stick on the ice; if serious injury is caused or blood is drawn it becomes a *major penalty* and a *game misconduct*.

dead puck: a *puck* that flies out of the *rink* or that a player has caught in his hand.

defensemen: two players who make up a team's defensive unit usually stationed in or near their *defensive zone* to help the *goalie* guard against attack; sometimes they lead an attack. The left *defenseman* covers the left half of the *rink*, the right defenseman plays to the right, but they can skate into each other's territory.

defensive line: consists of two *defensemen*.

defensive zone: the *zone* or area nearest a team's *goal* (the goal they are defending).

deflection: causing any pass or shot to stray from its intended course; a shot or pass that hits some object such as a stick or skate and goes into the *net* for a score or when a *goalie* hits the *puck* away.

deke or deking: a decoying or faking motion by the puck-carrier; the art of making a defensive player think you are going to pass or move in a certain direction when you are not. There are *shoulder dekes, stick dekes* and *head dekes*.

delayed penalty or delayed call: when an *official* raises his arm but does not blow his whistle, waiting to see the outcome of a play before calling a *penalty*; this is done so as not to penalize the non-offending team by stopping its momentum; a penalty that is delayed, and then not called, is *waved off* and play continues uninterrupted; also a penalty against the team that has only 4 players on the ice, which is assessed only when one of its players gets out of the penalty box.

delay of game: a *minor penalty* imposed on any player who purposely delays the game in any way, such as shooting or batting the *puck* outside the playing area or displacing the *goalpost* from its normal position.

double minor: a type of *minor penalty* given for certain accidental infractions that result in an injury to another player; penalty time of 4 minutes is served, double the time of a normal minor penalty.

drop pass: when a player simply leaves the *puck* behind for a teammate following him to pick up.

Eastern Conference: the renamed *Wales Conference* beginning with the 1993-94 season which contains the *Northeast* and *Atlantic Divisions*, formerly called the *Adams* and *Patrick Divisions*.

elbowing: a *minor penalty* which occurs when a player strikes his opponent with an elbow to impede his progress.

empty-net goal: a goal scored against a team that has *pulled the goalie*.

endboards: the *boards* at each end of the *rink*.

enforcer: also called the *policeman*; is usually the most penalized player on a team; he has the job of protecting his teammates from harm; generally a larger player who is not afraid of any fight.

exhibition game: a game not included in the *regular-season* schedule and which does not count in the *standings*; the *All-Star Game* or other games generally played before the season begins.

expansion: the addition of teams to the *NHL*.

expansion draft: a special arrangement to assist new *franchises* in obtaining players, where *expansion teams* choose players from other teams' *rosters*.

expansion team: a team that has been recently added to the *NHL*.

face mask: the protective mask worn by the *goalie*.

face-off: the method of starting play; the dropping of the *puck* by the *official* between the sticks of two opposing players standing one stick length apart with stick blades flat on the ice; used to begin each *period* or to resume play when it has stopped for other reasons.

face-off circles and spots: the various circular spots on the ice where an *official* and two players will hold a *face-off* to begin or to resume the action of the game; there are one blue and four red face-off circles located in the *neutral zone*; two red face-off circles are found at each end of the ice.

falling on the puck: a *minor penalty*, which occurs when a player other than the *goalie* closes his hand on the *puck*, deliberately falls on the puck, or gathers the puck under his body while lying on the ice.

feeding: passing the *puck*.

fighting: a *major penalty* which occurs when two or more players drop their sticks and gloves and fight; if a *referee* deems one player to be the instigator, that player gets a *game misconduct*; the *minor penalty* for a less severe pushing and shoving fight is called *roughing*.

flat pass: when a player passes the *puck* to a teammate along the surface of the ice.

flip pass: a pass by a player to a teammate that lifts the *puck* from the ice and sends it through the air, usually for the purpose of getting it over an opponent's stick.

flip shot: a shot in which a player cups the *puck* in his stick, then flips it with his wrists up off the ice towards the *goal*; this sometimes makes the puck harder to block.

forecheck: to *check* or harass an opponent who has the *puck* in his *defensive zone* and keep the opponents in their end of the *rink* while trying to regain control of the puck; usually done by the *forwards*.

forehand: a shot or pass taken from the right side of a right-handed player or from the left side of a left-handed player.

forward line or attacking line: consists of two *wings* (right and left) and a *center;* these three players play nearer the opponent's *goal* and are responsible for most of the scoring.

forwards: the three players who make up the attacking line or *forward line* of a team — the *center* and the *right* and *left wings.*

foul: any infraction of the rules that will draw a *penalty.*

franchise: a team; the legal arrangement that establishes ownership of a team.

freeze the puck: to hold the *puck* against the *boards* with the skate or stick in order to stop play briefly or gain a *face-off.*

full strength: when a team has its full complement of 6 players on the ice.

get the jump: to move fast and thereby get a good start on the opponents.

goal: provides one point; scored when a *puck* goes between the *goalposts* from the *stick* of an attacking player and entirely crosses the red line between the *goalposts;* also the informal term used to refer to the area made of the goalposts and the *net* guarded by the *goalie* and into which a puck must enter to score a point.

goal cage: a 6 foot wide by 4 foot high tubular steel frame consisting of a *cross bar* and two *goalposts* to which a *net* is attached.

goal crease: a semi-circular area with a 6 foot radius in front of the opening of the *goal;* denotes the playing area of the *goaltender* into which no player without the *puck* may enter.

goal line: the two-inch red line between the *goalposts* that stretches in both directions to the *sideboards.*

goalkeeper, goalie or goaltender: the heavily padded player who guards the *goal;* prevents opponents from scoring by stopping the *puck* any way he can.

goalposts: the metal bars that frame the area to which the *net* is attached which rests on the center of the *goal line* and between which a *puck* must pass to score a *goal.*

hat trick: three or more *goals* scored by a player in one game.

head deke: when a player drops his head as though moving one way and quickly moves in another to fake out the opponent.

high-sticking: a *minor penalty* which occurs when a player *checks* an opponent by carrying his *stick* above the normal height of his opponent's waist and hits, or menaces the opponent with it; if injury is caused it becomes a *major penalty*; if a *referee* determines that the raising of the stick was unintentional and no contact occurred, the *penalty* is only against the team and results in a *face-off*.

holding: a *minor penalty* which occurs when a player grabs and holds onto an opponent (or his stick) with his hands or arms to impede the opponent's progress.

holding the puck: see *falling on the puck*.

home team: the team in whose arena the game is being played; the team wearing the lighter uniforms.

hook check: a sweep of the *stick* low to the ice to take the *puck* from an opponent's stick.

hooking: a *minor penalty* which occurs when a player attempts to impede the progress of another player by hooking any part of the opponent's body with the blade of his *stick*; an illegal use of one's stick.

icing: a violation which occurs when the team in possession of the *puck* shoots it from behind the red *center line* across the opponent's *goal line* into the end of the *rink* (but not into the *goal*) and a member of the opposing team touches it first; results in a *face-off* in the offender's *defensive zone*; a *shorthanded* team cannot be called for icing.

interference: a *penalty* in hockey called when a player attempts to impede the motion of another player not in possession of the *puck*.

intermission: a fifteen-minute recess between each of the three *periods* of a hockey game.

kneeing: a *minor penalty* which occurs when a player uses a knee to hit his opponent in the leg, thigh or lower body.

lead pass: a pass sent ahead of a moving teammate designed to meet the player at the location he is headed.

lie: angle made by the shaft of the *stick* and the blade.

line change: the entire *forward line* and/or *defensive line* will be replaced at once, which puts players on the ice who work well together.

linesmen: the two *officials* on the ice, one toward each end of the *rink*, responsible for infractions of the rules concerning off-side plays at the *blue lines* or *center line* and for any *icing* violations; they conduct most of the *face-offs*, call *minor penalties* sometimes advise the *referee* concerning penalties, and separate players who are *fighting*; they wear black pants and an official league sweater, and are on *skates*.

major penalty: a type of individual *penalty* called for more serious infractions of the rules; of 5 minutes in duration whether or not the non-penalized team scores.

match-up: a pairing of players on opposing teams who will *cover* each other during the hockey game.

minor penalty: a type of *penalty* lasting 2 minutes; if the non-penalized team scores a *power play goal* during this time, the penalty ends immediately.

National Hockey League (NHL): a league started on November 22, 1917; currently contains 27 teams.

net: the *goal*; netting attached to the *goalposts* and frame of the goal to trap the *puck* when a goal is scored.

neutral zone: the area between the *blue lines*.

Norris Division: with the *Smythe Division* made up the *Campbell Conference* until the 1992-93 season; renamed the *Central Division* of the *Western Conference* in 1993.

officials: one *referee* and two *linesmen* on the ice calling infractions and handing out *penalties*; up to five off-ice *officials* including two *goal judges*, the *game timekeeper*, the *penalty timekeeper* and the *official scorer*.

offside pass: see *two-line pass*.

offsides: a violation which occurs when both *skates* of an attacking player cross the opponent's *blue line* preceding the *puck* into the *attacking zone* or when a pass crosses more than one line without being touched (*two-line pass*); this is one of the most common calls made in a hockey game.

on-the-fly: making player changes or *substitutions* while play is under way.

on the road: when an *NHL* team plays games away from its home arena.

open ice: that part of the ice that is free of opponents.

overtime: an additional *period* of play used to break a tie; see *sudden-death*.

passing: when one player uses his *stick* to send the *puck* to a teammate.

passout: a pass by an attacking player from behind his opponent's *net* or *goal line* to a teammate in front of the net.

Patrick Division: with the *Adams Division* made up the *Wales Conference* until the 1992-93 season; renamed the *Atlantic Division* of the *Eastern Conference* in 1993.

penalty: punishment of a player for a violation of the rules, resulting in suspension from the game for a period of time; 6 types exist: *minor, bench, major, misconduct, match* and *goalkeeper's penalties.*

penalty box: an area with a bench just off the ice, behind the *sideboards* outside the playing area, where penalized players serve their *penalty* time.

penalty killer: a player expert at *backchecking* and keeping or gaining control of a loose *puck* under difficult circumstances who is trained to break up a *power play* when his team is *shorthanded*.

penalty shot: a free shot awarded a player who was illegally interfered with, preventing him from a clear scoring opportunity; the shot is taken with only the *goalie* guarding against it.

periods: three 20-minute playing intervals separated by two *intermissions*.

points: the left and right positions taken by the *defensemen* of the attacking team, just inside the *blue line* of the *attacking zone*; also the term used to describe the defensemen playing at this location; also an individual statistic for players equal to their *goals* plus *assists*; also a team statistic used to determine team *standings* (2 points for each win and 1 point for each tie during the *regular season*).

poke check: a quick jab or thrust to the *puck* or opponent's *stick* to knock the puck away from him.

policeman: see *enforcer*.

power play: an attack by a team at *full strength* against a team playing one man (or two men) *shorthanded* because of a *penalty* (or penalties) which resulted in a player on the opposing team receiving *penalty-box* time.

puck: a black, vulcanized rubber disc, 1-inch thick and 3-inches in diameter, weighing between 5 ½ and 6 ounces used to play hockey; they are frozen to prevent excessive bouncing and changed throughout the game; can travel up to 120 miles per hour on a *slap shot*.

pulling the goalie: taking the *goalkeeper* off the ice and replacing him with a *forward*; leaves the *goal* unguarded so is only used as a last minute attempt to score.

ragging: retaining the *puck* by clever stickhandling; often used by a *shorthanded* team to kill time.

rebound: a *puck* that bounces off the *goalie's* body or equipment.

red line: the line that divides the length of the ice surface in half.

referee: the chief *official* in a hockey game, distinguished from the other officials by a red armband; he starts the game, calls most of the *penalties* and makes the final decision in any dispute; he is responsible for making sure the ice, the *nets* and the clock are in good condition; he wears black pants and an official league sweater; he is also on *skates*.

referee's crease: a semi-circular area, with a 10 foot radius, marked in red on the ice in front of the timekeepers' bench into which players may not follow a *referee*.

rink: the iced area inside the *boards* on which the game of hockey is played; it is 200 feet long by 85 feet wide with rounded corners.

rockered blades: used by professional ice hockey skaters; the gentle curve in a very sharp blade of an ice *skate* produced by rounding the toe and heel of the blade to make it easier for hockey players to turn quickly.

roster: a list of the players on a team.

roughing: a *minor penalty* which occurs when a fight between players is more of a pushing and shoving match; a less severe penalty than *fighting*.

rush: an individual or combined attack by a team in possession of the *puck*.

save: the act of a *goalie* in blocking or stopping a shot.

scramble: several players from both sides close together battling for possession of the *puck*.

screen shot: a shot on *goal* that the *goalie* cannot see because it was taken from behind one or more players from either team standing in front of the *net*.

shooting angle: the angle determined by the position of the shooting player in relation to the *goal* at the moment he shoots the *puck*.

shorthanded: a team with one or more players off the ice in the *penalty box* when the opponent has its full complement of 6 players; also a *power play* for the other team.

shot on goal (SOG): a scoring attempt that is successfully blocked or otherwise prevented by a *goalie*; a *save*.

shoulder deke: a quick move of the shoulder in one direction and the player in another to fake out the opponent.

sideboards: the *boards* along the sides of the *rink*.

slap shot: a shot in which the player raises his *stick* in a backswing, with his strong hand held low on the shaft and his other hand on the end as a pivot. Then as the stick comes down toward the *puck*, the player leans into the stick to put all his power behind the shot and add velocity to the puck; achieves an extremely high speed (up to 120 miles per hour) but is less accurate than a *wrist shot*.

slashing: a *minor penalty* which occurs when a player swings his *stick* from below the player's shoulder at an opponent to impede his motion, whether or not contact is made; if injury is caused it becomes a *major penalty* and a *game misconduct*.

sleeper: an attacking player who slips into the center or *neutral zone* behind the attacking *defensemen*; same as a floater or a hanger.

slow whistle: when an *official* waits to blow his whistle because of a *delayed offside* or *delayed penalty* call.

Smythe Division: with the *Norris Division* made up the *Campbell Conference* until the 1992-93 season; renamed the *Pacific Division* of the *Western Conference* in 1993.

solo: a *rush* by a player without assistance from a teammate.

spearing: a *major penalty* which occurs when a player illegally jabs, or even just attempts to jab, the point of his *stick* blade into another player's body; one of the most serious infractions a player can commit; results in an automatic *game misconduct*.

stick deke: when a player's *stick* is moved as though for a shot, but instead the player moves the *puck* past the defending player; done to fake out the opponent.

stickhandling: moving the *puck* along the ice with the *stick* blade.

substitution: occurs when a player comes off the bench to replace a player coming out of the game; can be made at any time and play does not need to stop.

sudden-death overtime: an *overtime period* that ends as soon as one team scores a *goal,* determining the winner and terminating the game.

sweep check: a *check* made by a player with one hand on the *stick,* and one knee so low it is practically on the ice, with the shaft and blade of the stick flat on the ice to take the *puck* away from an opponent.

third-man-in rule: the third man in a fight gets a *game misconduct penalty* and is out of the game for its duration; created to discourage players from jumping into a fight, even if they are only trying to break it up.

three-on-one: a type of *break* with three attackers coming in on one *defenseman;* this is a desperate situation.

three-on-two: a type of *break* with three attacking players skating against two defensive players.

trailer: a player who follows his teammate on the attack seemingly out of the action but actually in a position to receive a backward or *drop pass.*

tripping: a *minor penalty* which occurs when a player places his *stick* or a part of his body under or around the feet or legs of an opponent causing him to lose his balance; will also be called if a player kicks an opponent's *skates* out from under him, or uses a knee or leg to cause his opponent to fall.

two-line pass: a team violation occurring when a *puck* is passed across two or more lines without being touched; play is stopped for a *face-off;* a type of *offsides.*

two-on-one: a type of *break* with two attacking players skating against one defensive player.

two-on-two: a type of *break* with two attacking players skating against two defensive players.

under-led pass: a pass behind or to one side of a teammate, making it difficult for him to control the *puck*.

waffle pad: a large rectangular pad attached to the front of the *goalie's* stick hand.

Wales Conference: was one of the two confrences in the *NHL* consisting of the *Patrick* and *Adams Divisions* until the 1992-93 season. The other conference was *Campbell Conference*. These were renamed the *Eastern* and *Western Conferences* respectively in 1993.

wash out: a *goal* that is ruled invalid by the *refeeree* or the *waving off* of an infraction by the *linesmen*.

Western Conference: the renamed *Cambell Conference* begining with the 1993-94 season which contains the *Central* and *Pacific Divisions* (formerly the *Norris* and *Smythe Divisions* respectively).

wings: two players who flank the *center* on his right and left sides and, with him, make up the attacking unit or *forward line*.

wrist shot: a shot made using a strong flicking of the wrist and forearm muscles, with the *stick* blade kept on the ice; it is slower but more accurate than a *slap shot*.

Zamboni: the brand of machine used to clean the ice.

zones: three areas made up by the two *blue lines*; the *attacking zone* is the area farthest from the *goal* a player is defending; the *neutral zone* is the central area; the *defending zone* is the area where a player's goal is (the goal where his team's *goalie* is stationed).

INDEX

Bolded page numbers indicate a photograph, diagram or table.

A

Adams Award 82
Adams Division 53, **55**, 106
AHL iii
All-Star Game 76-77, 84, 106
All-Star Team 77, 84
American Hockey League, See *AHL*
Art Ross Trophy 79
assists 23, 28, 29, 63, **68**, **70**, **71**, 106
Atlantic Division 54, **55**, **66**
attacking zone 3, **6**, 19, **21**, 47, 106
awards 79-83

B

backchecking 24, 106
backhand shot 15, 106
Bailey, Ace 77, 105
Beliveau, Jean 71, 84, 92
benches **4**, 7, 38
best-of-seven series 57
Bettman, Gary 85, 103
blocking 16, 17, 24
blue lines 3, **4**, 33, 47, 106
boarding 37, 42, 106, **123**
boards 3, **4**, 22, 31, 106
body check 16, 48, 107
boots **9**
Bossy, Mike 68, 71, 72, 85, 97
Boucher, Frank 81
Bourque, Ray **69**, 80, 85-86
Bowman, Scotty 86
boxscore 65, **67**
break 47, 107
breakaway 47, 107
Bure, Pavel 86, 88

C

Calder, Frank 80, 103
Calder Memorial Trophy 80, 84
Campbell, Clarence 103
Campbell Bowl 58, 83
Campbell Conference 54, **55**, 83, 107
Canadian Hockey League v
captain 11, 33
caroms 46, 107
carrying the puck 35
center **21**, 23, 107
center face-off circle **4**, 6, 39, 107

center line 3, **4**, 34, 107
Central Division 54, **55**, **66**
Central Hockey League, See *CHL*
charging 37, 42, 107, **123**
checking 16, **17**, 24, 50, **108**
CHL iv
choosing sides 18
Clancy, Frank ("King") 81
clear the puck 52, 108
Coffey, Paul 68, 69, 71, 72, 86, 86-87
Colonial Hockey League v
Commissioner, NHL 85, 103
conferences ii, 53-**55**, 76
Conn Smythe Trophy 80, 84
cover 46, 108
cross bar **5**, 108
cross-checking 37, **43**, 108, **123**
cut down the angle 50, **51**

D

defending zone 3, **6**, **21**, 24, 52, 108
defense 16, 50
defensemen, left and right **21**, 23-24,
       79, 84, 108
defensive line **21**, 108
defensive zone **6**, 14, **21**
deflections 49, 108
deking 47-48, 109
delay of game 40, 43, 109
Dionne, Marcel 68, 69, 87
diving 37
division leader 56
divisions ii, 53-**55**, 56
double minors, See *penalty, double*
       minor
draft, NHL, See *NHL draft*
drop pass 16, 109
Dryden, Ken 87
dumping the puck 47, **48**
Durnan, Bill 80
Dutton, Red 103

E

East Coast Hockey League, See *ECHL*
Eastern Conference 53, 54, **55**, 58, **66**,
       83, 109
ECHL iv
elbowing 37, 43, 109, **123**

119

empty-net goal 52, 64, 109
enforcer 27, 109
equipment **8-10**
equipment violations 12
Esposito, Phil **68**, **69**, 73, 79, 87, 88, 91, 97
Esposito, Tony 72, 88, 93
expansion 53-54, 81, 109
expansion draft 74, 110
expansion team ii, 74, 110

F

face mask 11, 12, 102, 110
face-off **18**, 23, 30, 33, 36, 43, 110
face-off circles/spots **4**, 6, 18, 19, 39, 110
falling on the puck 38, 43, 110
Federov, Sergei 88-89
fighting 38, 39, 43, 44, 110, **124**
five-hole 48-**49**
flat pass 15, 110
flip pass 15, 110
flip shot 15, 110
Forsberg, Peter 89, 100
forward line **21**, 22, 23, 111
forwards 81, 84, 111
freezing the puck 19, 26, 111
full strength 42, 111

G

game summaries 65, **67**
Gartner, Mike 89-90
gloves **10**, 11, 25
goal 2, 13, 23, 28, 29, 63, **67**, **68**, **69**, **71**, 79, 111
goal cage **4**, **5**, 19, 111
goal crease **4**, **5**, 7, 24, 28, 32, 49, 111
goal judges **4**, 30, 31
goal lines 3, **4**, 28, 32, 35, 111
goalie 5, 9, 16, **21**, 22, 24-26, **25**, 40, 48-**49**, 50, 79-80, 81, 84, 111
goalkeeper, See goalie
goalposts **5**, 28, 111
goals-against 64, **66**
goals-against average 64, **73**
goals for **66**
Gretzky, Wayne **68**, **69**, **70**, **71**, **72**, 79, 82, 85, 87, 88, 89, **90**-91, 92, 93, 96, 97, 100, 105

H

Hall, Glenn 72, 73, 92

Hall of Fame, Canada 78, 79, 84
Hall of Fame, United States 78
hand pass 43
hand signals, officials' 30, **123-125**
Hart Memorial Trophy 79
Harvey, Doug 80, 92
Hasek, Dominic **73**, 80, 92-93
hat trick 28, 100, 111
helmets **10**, 11
high-sticking 35, 37, 43, 112, **123**
holding 37, 43, 112, **123**
holding the puck 112
hooking 37, **44**, 112, **124**
Howe, Gordie **68**, **69**, **72**, 79, 87, 88, 91, 93-**94**, 95, 101, 103
Hull, Bobby 68, 94-**95**, 101
Hull, Brett **69**, **71**, 95-**96**

I

icing 31, **34**, 35, 52, 112, **124**
IHL iii
injury 14, 19, 30
interference 37, 44, 112, **124**
intermission 13, 112
International Hockey League, See IHL

J

Jagr, Jaromir 85, 96
Jennings Award 81

K

Kariya, Paul 96-97
kicking the puck 14
kill the penalty 42, 52
King Clancy Memorial Trophy 81
kneeing 44, 112, **124**
Kurri, Jari 68, 69, 71, 72, 97, 100

L

Lady Byng Trophy 81, 84
Lafleur, Guy 82, 97-98
lead pass 16, 112
leaving the bench illegally 37
LeClair, John 98
Lemieux, Mario **68**, **69**, **70**, **71**, 79, 82, 96, 98-**99**, 100, 105
Lindros, Eric 89, 98, 100
line changes 22, 112
linesmen 30-31, **67**, 113
Lord Stanley 59

M

Major League Roller Hockey, See *MLRH*
Masterton Trophy 81
match-ups 46, 86, 113
Maurice "Rocket" Richard Award 79, 103
Messier, Mark 68, 69, 71, 72, 91, 97, 100
Mikita, Stan 68, 79, 101
minor leagues ii-v
misconduct, See *penalty, misconduct*
MLRH vi
Montreal Canadiens 41-42, 53, 59, 60, 79, 80, 84, 86, 87, 88, 92, 95, 97, 98, 102, 103, 105
Most Valuable Player (MVP) 80, 84

N

National Hockey League (NHL) ii, 113
net 3, **5**, 48-**49**, 113
neutral zone 3, 5, **6**, 19, 113
NHL Draft 74-75
NHL Players' Association (NHLPA) 82
NHL teams 53-**55**
Norris Division 54, **55**, 113
Norris Trophy 79-80, 84
Northeast Division 54, **55**, **66**
Northwest Division 54, **55**, **66**

O

offense 14, 46-49
official scorer 7, 28, 30, 32
officials 28, 30, 47, 113
officials' hand signals, See *hand signals, officials'*
offsides, delayed 34
offsides 31, 33-**34**, 113, **124**
on-the-fly 22, 113
onsides 34
open player 47, 50
origins of hockey 1
Orr, Bobby **70**, 80, **101**-102, 102
overtime ii, 13, 31, 114

P

Pacific Division 54, **55**, **66**
passing 15-16, 114
Patrick Award 82
Patrick Division 54, **55**, 114
Pearson Award 82
penalties, coincidental 40
penalties, delayed 36, 41, 109, **123**
penalties, double minor 37, 109
penalty 7, 30, 33-45, **67**, 114
penalty, bench 33, 38
penalty, game or match 33, 38
penalty, game misconduct 39
penalty, goalie 40
penalty, individual 33, **42-45**
penalty, major 33, 37-38, 113
penalty, minor 31, 33, 37, 92, 113
penalty, misconduct 30, 33, 38-39, **124**
penalty, team 33-35
penalty benches 35
penalty box **4**, 7, 30, 35, 114
penalty killers 22, 26, 42, 114
penalty minutes 63
penalty shot ii, 32, 33, 39-40, 114
periods 13, 31, 114
PIM, See *penalty minutes*
Plante, Jacques 72, 73, 80, 102
playoff brackets **58**
playoffs, See *Stanley Cup Playoffs*
plus/minus 63-64, 82
Plus/Minus Award 82
points iii, 2, 13, **21**, 24, 29, 51, 56, 63, 65, **69**, **70**, **72**, 79, 114
policeman 27, 114
possession 14
post-season 13, 56, 74
Potvin, Denis 71, 72, 102-103
power play 22, 41-42, 50-52, 63, 92, 115
power play goals 63
power play set up 50-52
President's Trophy 82
Presidents, NHL 80, 103
Prince of Wales Trophy 58, 83
Professional Hockey Writers' Association 79, 80-81
puck **8**, 9, 115
puck, dead 19, 108
puck, frozen 19, 108
puck carrier 14, 47-48
pulling the goalie 52, 115

R

realignment 54, 57
records, individual **68-73**
referee 28, 30, 33, **67**, 115
referee's crease **4**, 7, 30, 115
regular season ii, 13, 56, 71
regulation game 13

RHI vi
Richard, Maurice ("Rocket") 79, 91, 92, 103
rink 3, **4**, 115
roller hockey vi
Roller Hockey International, See *RHI*
rookie v, 80
rosters ii, 115
roughing 37, 44, 115, **124**
rounds, draft 74
rounds, playoff 56-58
Roy, Patrick 73, 103
rush 47, 115

S

Sakic, Joe 103-104
save 26, 63, 116
Sawchuck, Terry 72, 73, 80, 104
screen the goalie 49, 116
seeded 57
Selanne, Teemu 69, 85, 104-105
Selke Award 81-82
shooting **14**-15
shootout ii, iii, iv
Shore, Eddie 76, 105
shorthanded 20, 22, 35-36, 38, 42, 50, 52, 63, 116
shorthanded goals 63
shot on goal 26, 47, 63, **67**, 116
shutouts 64, **72**, **73**
skates **9**, **10**
slap shot **14**, 15, 95, 116
slashing 37, 44, 116, **125**
slow whistle 116, **125**
Smythe Division 54, **55**, 116
SO, See *shutout*
SOG, See *shots on goal*
Southeast Division 54, **55**, **66**
spearing 38, **45**, 117, **125**
standings 56, 65-**66**
Stanley Cup ii, 58-60, **59**
Stanley Cup Finals 57-58, 74, 80
Stanley Cup history 59-60
Stanley Cup losers **61-62**
Stanley Cup Playoffs ii, 13, 56-59, 80
Stanley Cup winners **61-62**
starting lineup 21, 38, 46, 76
Stastny, Peter 104
statistician 30, 32
statistics, individual 63-64, **67**
statistics, team **65-67**
Stein, Gil 103
stick check 16

sticks **8**-9
stopping play 19
substitutions 22, 38, 117
sudden-death ii, iv, 13, 117
Sunshine Hockey League v

T

third-man-in rule 39, 117
Thompson, Tiny 72, 73
time-outs 14
timekeepers 7, 30, 31-32
timekeepers' table 4, 7, 30
too many men on ice 22, 38, 45
tripping 37, 45, 117, **125**
trophies 79-83
two-line pass **34**, 117

U

UHL v
uniforms 9-11, **10**
uniforms, goalie 11
United Hockey League, See *UHL*
unsportsmanlike conduct 38, **125**

V

Vezina, Georges 80, 105
Vezina Trophy 80, 84, 105
video goal judge 30, 32

W

waffle pad 11, 118
Wales Conference 53, 54, **55**, 83, 118
wash-out 118, **125**
WCHL v
West Coast Hockey League, See *WCHL*
Western Conference 53, 54, **55**, 58, **66**, 83, 118
Western Professional Hockey League, See *WPHL*
WHA 54, 84
win-loss-tie record 56, **66**
wings, left and right **21**, 23, 118
World Hockey Association, See *WHA*
WPHL v
wrist shot 15, 118

Y

Yzerman, Steve 69, 105

Z

Zamboni 12, 13, 118
Ziegler, John 103

OFFICIALS' HAND SIGNALS

BOARDING: pounding a closed fist into the open palm of the opposite hand (see page 42).

CHARGING: clenched fists rotating around each other in front of the chest (see page 42).

CROSS-CHECKING: two clenched fists extending out from the chest in a forward and backward motion (see page 42).

DELAYED CALLING OF PENALTY: one arm extended up in the air by the *referee* with whistle in mouth, then pointing once to the guilty player (see page 41).

ELBOWING: tapping the elbow with the opposite hand (see page 42).

HIGH-STICKING: both hands clenched, held one just above the other at forehead level (see page 43).

HOLDING: clasping one wrist with the other hand, just in front of the chest (see page 43).

HOOKING: tugging motion with both arms, as though pulling something toward himself (see page 44).

ICING: arms folded against the chest (see page 35).

INTERFERENCE: fists closed with arms crossed and stationary in front of his chest (see page 44).

KNEEING: slapping the knee with one hand, both skates on the ice (see page 44).

MISCONDUCT: both hands placed on the hips, then pointing to the penalized player (see page 38-39).

OFFSIDES: *linesman* points at the *blue line* (see page 33-34).

ROUGHING, FIGHTING: a thrusting motion of the arm extending from the side (see page 44, 43).

SLASHING: a chopping motion with the edge of one hand on the opposite forearm (see page 45).

SLOW WHISTLE: a linesman's non-whistle arm held straight up; lowered the instant the puck crosses the line back into the neutral zone.

SPEARING: a jabbing motion with both hands in front of the body (see page 45).

TRIPPING: hitting right leg with right hand below the knee, both skates on the ice (see page 45).

WASH-OUT (REFEREE): both arms swung laterally across the body with palms facing down to disallow a goal.

WASH-OUT (LINESMEN): both arms swung laterally across the shoulders with palms facing down when there is no *icing* or no *offsides*.

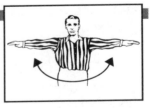

UNSPORTSMANLIKE CONDUCT: using both hands to form the letter T in front of the chest (see page 38).

ORDER FORM

Order any of the following Spectator Guides:

Title	Qty	Price	Total
Basketball Made Simple		$9.95	
Football Made Simple		$9.95	
Ice Hockey Made Simple		$9.95	
Soccer Made Simple		$9.95	
How To Win a Sports Scholarship		$19.95	
Subtotal			
Add $2.50 per book for shipping & handling ($2.95 for Scholarship book) → S&H			
Add $2.00 for rush delivery Rush Delivery			
Sales Tax (CA)			
Total			

Order by phone toll-free: **800-247-8228**

or send form to : First Base Sports, Inc.
P.O. Box 1731
Manhattan Beach, CA 90267-1731

Name _____

Street Address _____

City _____

State _____ Zip _____

Phone No. _____

Method of Payment:

Check ☐ or Charge: VISA ☐ Master Card ☐

Card # _____ Exp. Date (required)_____

Signature _____ H/98